IN SEARCH OF ULTIMATES

IN SEARCH OF ULTIMATES

By

William D. Streng

AUGSBURG PUBLISHING HOUSE
Minneapolis   **Minnesota**

IN SEARCH OF ULTIMATES

Scripture quotations are from the Revised Standard Version of the Bible, copyright 1946 and 1952 by the Division of Christian Education of the National Council of Churches.

Acknowledgments for quotations used by permission appear at end of the book.

Manufactured in the United States of America

TO

MY CHILDREN

WHO ARE ALSO

SEARCHING

PREFACE

The basic theme of this book is inescapable: One can evade ultimate questions by ignoring them, but that is an answer also.

Having dealt with church people through the years, I have been convinced that many are desperately searching to un-clutter much of what is offered by the church and to find, after sober inquiry, what is really essential. And unless we offer help in this area for adults, many serious and searching minds will be increasingly alienated from the Christian faith.

I surmise that some may be shocked at much that I have written in these pages. In shocking I take no pleasure. But I, too, have had to change during the more than three decades of my ministry. I simply appeal to candid and open minds to restudy traditional presentations and consider afresh what in these days of catastrophe needs to be underscored.

My hope is that these pages for adults can be used profitably to discuss informally with those who are curious about the Christian faith, or those who are interested in a refresher course, the great affirmations of the Christian faith in a contemporary setting. The former group may wish to develop in greater detail the first chapters of this book, while the second group could concentrate more fully on aspects of renewal. Smaller cells may wish to use these pages as guidelines for discussion in the living room. Selectivity of these for discussion is, of course, the privilege of any group which uses these pages—in fact, both time and background will determine which items for discussion will be of value to the individuals in that particular setting.

The only assumption I make in these pages is that you are interested in ultimates. The issue is there, you know, and we have to make a decision concerning it. The major purpose of these pages is to help you make an intelligent and responsible decision. It may be that we have to sing a requiem today for a God who is dead, or we may be on the verge of a rebirth of religious faith. To evade the issue is impossible.

In this area one usually receives two kinds of answers.

Some are convinced that the church has all the answers, even to the most involved problems of our day. If we know enough about the Bible, such people assume, then we can press the right button on a sort of spiritual computer, and we are sure to get a clear and concise answer to our inquiries.

Others have come to the conclusion that the Christian church is in such a state of confusion that no real answers are forthcoming at all. Do we not read with mechanical regularity about bishops and other churchmen who seem to deny some of the basic tenets of the Christian faith? Is it not enough in our day to have a kind of "religion-in-general"—in fact, is there anything else available? Is it respectable at all to have any kind of faith that is passionate and particular when no one, exactly no one, seems to be sure about anything anymore?

The author is convinced that these are not the only alternatives—a sort of all or nothing. The Christian church, as a rule, does not lay claim to either position.

Hence the format of these pages does not follow the catechetical approach of question and answer or chapter by chapter presentation, though the purpose is the same. Not only is the Bible not a monolithic body of organized truths, but the author is also convinced that faith in God is more than objective knowledge of the facts of salvation. Every attempt of that kind hopelessly misses God and his revelation. Faith is directed toward the why of God's revelation and not primarily toward the what, since the why leads to the question: Whom can this help? If we insist that everyone study the same scripture verse, we are like the pharmacist who gives everyone penicillin no matter what the ailment may be.

Hence also the heavy emphasis in these pages on theses, quotations, questions, for without participation there is no communication; without anxiety there is no learning. In the polemical and patriarchal approach of the typical catechism, truth was understood as definable and transmissible, while docility in listening was taken as acceptance and devotion. To continue this kind of approach will only sow more seeds of rejection as far as ultimates are concerned.

The new mentality understands truth as the eventful resonance of life with Life, for there is much of value in the insistence of one of our contemporaries that education is not instruction; it is discovery. These pages also try to take seriously the suggestion of Dr. Hans Hoekendijk that a modern catechism would have to "lead us on a course of thinking things through with question after question after question, thus inviting us to search things out for ourselves," even as a modern textbook in American history does not tell students what conditions prevailed in Nebraska in 1850 but has them search and discover how they would live if they had moved there during that period. In that sense the Christian faith or its alternative is a search for every new generation and individual.

Will you come with me as we attempt a search for basic issues, for ultimates, provided there are some?

These pages are concerned with the jugular and not with the capillaries. There is worth in the latter, but the former, it seems to me, is more vital at this stage of our history. It is extremely difficult—some maintain it is impossible—to formulate a list of first principles from which a viable faith may be forged, sustained by traditional Christianity and yet with some degree of relevance for this moment. But perfection is gained, according to a noted artist, not when there is nothing to add but when there is nothing more to take away.

Take away they did. And I must thank some of my seminary students who gleefully and relentlessly pruned out large sections of my original manuscript as "totally irrelevant," and Mrs. Wm. D. Streng who accomplished the same purpose in a more gentle manner, and Mrs. Leone Hoefflin for going beyond the call of duty in the detailed work of preparing page after page for print.

There are times in this discussion when you will be able to correct me, but there is never a time when you or I can evade the difficult decision concerning ultimates. We shall make mistakes in many decisions, but if we fail to decide, we shall always be wrong. And even though every decision we make is based on a previous error, it has to be made to the best of our ability. Whether we are in the organized church or whether we have preferred not to be associated with it, the reasons for our decision ought to be clear. It may be that by a renewed search for ultimates we can become a bit more truly human in our response.

WILLIAM D. STRENG

CONTENTS

PAGE

Chapter I.   — Condemned to Meaning 1

Chapter II.   — Viable Alternatives 8

Chapter III.   — Who Has the Lantern? 16

Chapter IV.   — God 25

Chapter V.   — Planned History 35

Chapter VI.   — Bearded Tradition 44

Chapter VII.   — Has the Church Betrayed Christ? 57

Chapter VIII. — Dialogue Without Prejudice 68

Chapter IX.   — Inside the Cup 82

Chapter X.   — Renewal of Man 95

Chapter XI.   — Capitulation or Revolution? 104

Chapter XII.   — Anatomy of Futility 118

Chapter XIII. — Tell Me About My Home 126

Acknowledgments 139

Indexes 147

Picture Section .... following 36

CHAPTER ONE

CONDEMNED
TO MEANING

Where do you start in discussing religion? The answers given are many and extremely varied. One may keep referring to the church or to his own local parish; another refers to the Bible; another to tradition, and still another to his favorite catechism. And so the confusion continues while a world is racing toward catastrophe.

Maybe the answer is simply to avoid all discussion. With countless religious debates in our history, which seem to have been positively useless and even harmful, why continue along a line which has proved futile?

Anyhow, religion is more, much more, than discussion. Why not be content with serving mankind and leave theology to the experts? Is it not true, as a motto states above the portal of an elegant church building in Florence, Italy: "Where love is there is God"?

This, too, has been attempted with all sincerity during our history. But really now, can there be faith without content? We cannot make decisions in a vacuum. There are certain basic doctrinal affirmations which constitute the conceptual expression of an attitude called "faith." If I practice love, why and whom shall I serve and how shall I proceed? How much must I know in order to be a follower of Christ? Alert young people today are repeating with mechanical regularity the assertion: "I believe in Christ, but I certainly don't care for the organized church." Are these alternatives valid?

The problem is intensified by the tendency to add further material and countless stipulations to the original minimum and essential content. In the first century it was sufficient to base one's life on the conviction that "Jesus is Lord." Why then have the churches added countless strictures to this simple affirmation by maintaining that we must believe in Mary's assumption or in the verbal inspiration of the Bible; that we must promise not to drink alcoholic beverages, or that we must assert that the bread and wine of the Sacrament are actually the Body and Blood of Christ?

The problem is further intensified when the basic affirmations of the Gospels are extended to such areas of human action as the social and the political, the economic and the ethical. Must I agree when my church body or an alliance such as the World Council of Churches solemnly passes a resolution for or against abortion or in favor of capital punishment? Or if some prominent church prelates insist that our country ought to engage in war while other churchmen oppose such brutality, is there any way out of such ambiguity? Should or should not the church be engaged in these areas?

This sort of process seems to be inevitable; history offers countless instances of this kind of development—namely, that a revelatory act of God was covered with traditional practices and the dust of centuries so that the original was hardly recognizable. The Decalogue (the Ten Commandments) was a gift of divine favor to help a nation grow in responsibility and maturity. But succeeding generations tried to preserve these commandments in alcohol by codifying every concrete situation— you dare not work on holy days, sex is evil, you must pray certain hours of the day, etc.

A similar extension has grown to almost monumental proportions in Christianity. A simple meal in an Upper Room given by Christ for the comfort and encouragement of his friends has developed into an elaborate ritual with precise procedures and harsh restrictions stating that only certain ones can come to this altar, ignoring the fact that Christ is the host and not we. From a church which despite glaring weaknesses exulted in serving and loving what we have today?

But how can we distinguish the essence of the faith from the merely accidental, the substance from the formulation? How do we separate what is permanent and unchangeable from the ethical and social assertions which, because they are responses to specific historical situations, are destined to become stale?

This tension exists already in the Bible. In fact, it is at the basis of one of our major problems. Does one laugh or cry when all statements of the Bible are placed on the same level of importance? Must one read a chapter a day or know the weight of Absalom's hair (still better, the conflicting weights of his hair)? Sometimes we discuss with equal seriousness the blacktopping of a church yard and the plight of millions of lives in India as if both of these were basic to Christian discipleship. Is there no question of priorities here? Is there no hierarchy of truth? At the other extreme one may listen to a profound discussion of the dialectic (tension) between law and Gospel and imagine that one has engaged in something God-pleasing.

In order to lessen this tension, to draw the lines a bit more clearly between the essentials of the Christian faith and its accoutrements, to decipher what is of enduring value and what elements, incorporated by tradition, are no longer immediately relevant in our day, we are obliged to carry on a permanent reflection and meditation on the meaning of human existence as this is revealed to us by God. This places us always under judgment, including the church.

Such an effort is required doubly in our day, since new lines of battle are being drawn in the church in every denomination among men. Simply to decide to join the ranks of the conservatives in order to be faithful to what "the Bible says," to confessions and traditions with a heavy emphasis on conversion, or to support the "liberals" who claim loyalty to personal, contextual, contemporary "truth" is basically to evade the issue. Worse still, to defend a set of theological positions may be a modern way of selling indulgences.

The coming struggle will not be between conservative and liberal—we will not be faced with that alternative. Nor will the immediate future continue the controversy between Roman

Catholics and Protestants. The controversy as it seems to be developing now is the conflict over traditional versus experimental forms of witness, worship, and behavior. On both sides there will be Roman Catholics and Lutherans and Methodists and Jews. The struggle can roughly be divided between those who favor greater involvement in social issues and those who feel that the church should stick to the problem of helping individuals find salvation.

Responsible people find it difficult to reach a satisfying answer when confronted by this decision. But face it we must.

For Further Discussion

1. A renowned Dutch Roman Catholic theologian maintains that one of the most heretical acts in which we can engage today is to recite the traditional, historic creeds. What is he trying to say? Do you agree?

2. Is it proper to accuse the church of engaging in "blasphemous blah-blah," of being a "cult of triviality"?

3. What is the nature of the desire for change among Christians?

4. How would you react to this statement: "The church should return to its basic purpose—leading unsaved souls to Christ. The individual should be involved in social issues, but the church should stay clear of these issues."

5. In the Gospel records, does Jesus speak more often of faith or of love? Why?

6. Does this statement say anything to us: "Faith and freedom are the two most important aspects of man's fundamental need: love. Where love reigns, faith and freedom follow. When love dies, faith and freedom die also."[1]

7. How has your parish solved the question of priorities?

8. Which way do you lean in your decisions concerning basic issues?

9. Are any experiments overdue in your parish, in your individual life? Now? How?

10. What problems in this area remain for you? Do real Christians ever have periods of doubt and despair?

11. Have you seen any indications of the truth of this assertion: "The greatest overall achievement of the Second Vatican Council was its conscious proclamation of the fact that Christianity is an adult religion, and therefore a way of life that can be adequately understood and lived by those who have 'come of age'."[2]

12. Evaluating the old type of evangelism campaigns Cecil Northcott maintains: "This, I submit, is a debasement of the central concern of the Bible, which is centered on the encounter of God with man and the perfect meeting of God and man in Christ. Personal salvation is not the overwhelming fact in the Bible. To isolate this truth is a disservice to evangelism and marks its abdication."[3]

13. What does this say to us: "The question *cannot* be: how do we communicate the Gospel so that others will accept it. For this there is no method. To communicate the Gospel means putting it before the people so that they are able to decide for or against it. The Christian Gospel is a matter of decision. It is to be accepted or rejected. All that we who communicate this Gospel can do is to make possible a genuine decision. Such a decision is one based on understanding and on partial participation.

"We all know the pain we suffer when we meet people who reject the Gospel, although they have no authority for rejecting it, or meet other people who were not able to make a genuine decision about it, since the Gospel was never properly communicated to them. Another experience which is but slightly less painful is to meet those who have accepted it without ever having been able to make a decision about it because it never was a matter of doubt. It came to them as a matter of habit, custom or social contact. This the Gospel can never be.

"True communication of the Gospel means making possible a definite decision for or against it. . . . Whether we shall succeed in this nobody knows. This is the risk we must take."[4]

14. We may have to read the entire book to understand what a New Testament scholar means with the assertion, "the contents of the revelation are mysteriously inseparable from the forms in which they are conveyed."[5] What variety one finds in the Bible's method of communication; there are parables, sayings, epistles, etc. Why? Did Paul regret that he had to put his message into writing? (See Galatians 4:20.) Luther also regrets that books had to be written to convey the Christian Gospel, for this is a breach with the Holy Spirit. Why did not Jesus write books? How does the author of Ecclesiastes groan at the weariness of many words? And yet, do words have any power, words like: "The court finds you guilty" or "I baptize thee" or even the ranting statements of dictators?

15. Jesus' teaching, or any Spirit-filled communication, always calls for response, not memorization or persuasion or transcription. Since I cannot decide without information, I need content, theology, language. The parables of Christ are excellent illustrations. They are good pedagogical strategy, but they are more— they are interesting, but that is not why Christ related them; they are brief, but they are not mere illustrations pulled out of his file. They confront with ultimate choices. How?

16. Why is confrontation or encounter so vital? "In both Testaments, then, everything turns upon an encounter of man with God." By encounter, engagement, confrontation is meant "the moment when God acts in or upon the life of an individual and the individual faces the responsibility to respond."[6]

17. The relation of God to man is pictured in the Bible as king—subject; husband—wife; master—slave; father—son; brother —brother, and others. Is encounter central and constant and basic to all of these? We are addressed and must answer.

18. Do you know of a better word than confrontation to express this encounter? Our relationship to God is deeper and broader than sheer up-againstness. Nor does confrontation, unless it is explained, include the riches of God's steadfast love. Maybe we ought to begin with confrontation and lead up to—what?

19. Have we asked the important questions in this chapter?

Books for Suggested Reading

(listed in a progression from easy to difficult)

1. Daniel Jenkins, *Beyond Religion*. Westminster, 1962.

2. James D. Smart, *The Old Testament in Dialogue with Modern Man*. Westminster, 1964

3. Roger Hazelton, *New Accents in Contemporary Theology*. Harper, 1960.

4. Amos N. Wilder, *The Language of the Gospel*. Harper, 1964.

5. Paul Tournier, *The Meaning of Persons*. Harper, 1957.

6. Huston Smith, *Condemned to Meaning*. Harper, 1965.

7. Rosemary Radford Ruether, *The Church Against Itself*. Herder and Herder, 1967.

CHAPTER TWO

VIABLE ALTERNATIVES

Where do you start in matters of religion? We did not answer that question in the previous chapter. Yet unless we see the possibilities available, much of the tension among Christians will remain a blur for us.

In matters of religion one can begin with God or with man. Ideally these should converge, especially if we restrict ourselves to essentials.

Historically the approach has recently been largely limited to an emphasis on God and his revelation. "The Bible says" is for some basic to any discussion and should, according to their convictions, be the opening statement in any dialogue concerning the faith.

Traditionally many of us have been nurtured on this approach. We studied the Bible book by book whether the lessons were particularly meaningful or not.

But this paternalistic type of education, consisting of a packaged sequence of suggested courses, may well be passé in our day. As educators have pointed out, this kind of education forces the student into a passive situation and hardly ever opens him up to the possibility of being a self-starter. Assertions gaining credence in educational circles now are, "We are entering the new age of education that is programmed for discovery rather than instruction. . . . More and more we turn from the content of messages to study total effect."[1]

Closely related to paternalistic education is the "monologue" style of communication: a teacher lecturing about the Word of God to passive listeners who should be eager to hear what "the Bible says." Such presentations have aptly been called an "exercise in dinosaurism." Unless such teaching is supplemented by "dialogue" in small face-to-face groups, it denies us an opportunity to learn in terms of our own words and meanings what relevance all this has for us. Often the church has given the impression of sitting on the heights, impervious to the needs of men.

Is Reality Good?

To forestall this kind of sterile approach it may be best to begin asking questions about ourselves. Albert Camus speaks of the "hopeless gulf between the question of man and the silence of the world" *(The Rebel)*.

I quote this perceptive author, for he has tried to get an answer from the world, from education, from philosophers, as to why we are here. Why is there something rather than nothing? All these people walking around—some we love and some we've never met —does their existence have any meaning? One of these days they shall all be gone—and I will no longer be here either. Was it all a bubble without any permanent content?

Who am I anyway and why do I exist and what does it mean to be a human being? Right now I'm not much interested in putting up a new church building from which to be buried or in a more modern translation of the Bible which I hardly ever read, but I would like to know whether life is simply a tangled mess veneered with artificial smiles or whether there is some unifying center that brings at least a little order out of this chaos. Is reality good or bad or indifferent?

It is time—our times demand it—that we approach questions of reality with honesty and freshness and candor and penetration. And any question that's worth asking ought to be asked whether we can find an answer for it or not. This concerns my existence, my identity, my worth as an individual; frankly, I know of nothing more important.

Is the world really silent when we ask: Who am I? What is man? Is life meaningful? Certainly we are not the first ones to ask this question.

Nor has the world been altogether silent. Countless great minds have speculated on the meaning of existence. Even a summary of their thoughts is not very useful unless we insist on evading the issue by making a list of answers from others. That may be a useful academic exercise, but most of us have taken enough notes on lectures which we have filed away for good.

I, too, am lonely. I am lonely in the midst of a bustling city where everyone rushes past my door as if he were really going somewhere or running away from something. I am lonely in a restaurant when I often ache for fellowship, but no one dares to talk to anyone else. I am lonely in my family circle where no one, exactly no one, really understands me.

The scientist and the psychiatrist can, of course, analyze me and make life intensely interesting. What is more scintillating than to observe the scientist in making new discoveries? One simply gasps at the immensity of our expanding universe. I read somewhere that the closest star is over four light-years away. How far is that? I'll copy it down—that would be 186,000 times the number of seconds in a minute times the number of minutes in an hour times the number of hours in a day times the number of days in a year. The answer comes out to 5,865,696,000,000 miles. The closest star is over four times that far. If a space ship could travel at a speed of two million miles an hour, it would take over 1,300 years for it to reach the closest star. Of course, some of the farther stars are millions of light years away. In addition, astronomers are fairly certain that just one of our galaxies, like the Milky Way, has at least 100 billion stars in it.

So what? Who am I and do I have any significance in this vast universe? Does anyone ever look at me with a telescope? And I have health and family and friends and food. What about the youngster with leukemia and the old widower by his window for whom life is so "daily"?

Maybe the social scientist can be of help. No question about it, he can analyze us and practically predict what kind of person or culture we shall have if certain factors are present in our training and environment. In addition, today's advances in biology, especially the growing understanding of the genetic code, may make it possible to produce the kind of man we want. But who determines whose sperm is to be deposited in a sperm bank or whose ova shall be chosen? Someone must guard these, but who guards the guardians?

Or who is not interested in psychology? At least the psychologist is concerned about me and other human beings. He can help me understand myself, my motives and drives and aspirations. But even one of the best of them admits freely, "No amount or depth of psychological insight can ever take the place of the act, of the commitment, of the leap. It can lead to it, prepare it, make it possible—and this is the legitimate function of psychoanalytic work. But it must not try to be a substitute for the responsible act of commitment, an act without which no real change occurs in a human being."[2]

Question of Priorities

Those are words of wisdom. The psychiatrist can analyze— even prepare for an act of commitment—but the real change must occur through the effort and prompting of another.

Of whom? Certainly not from an authoritarian church which tells me to recite a creed and sit in church on Sunday morning. And I hope it isn't necessary, in order to take the leap of commitment of which Erich Fromm speaks, to be forced to believe against my better judgment that the world was created in six days, that every word in the Bible is historically accurate, that the Jews are still cursed because they killed Jesus, and that one little denomination has more of the truth than all the others put together.

Honest and pious and devout people are convinced that this is the only correct and valid kind of answer. The sincerity and fervor of many of them are beyond question.

But there is an alternative, equally honest and valid for others. There is a possibility to retain that which is permanent in the Christian tradition and still saturated with relevance for our day. Some of the applications may change as conditions vary, but priorities remain the same. It may be that for theology to have a rebirth we had best start with the world, its hopes and problems and aspirations. We may also discover that discussion which had become arid will suddenly have new water flowing in old channels.

At least we ought to be aware of these viable options. And since the latter approach is least known to us it is incumbent upon us that we try to discover what its salient features are at this moment of our history, fully cognizant of the fact that the knowledge explosion in theology is so broad and intense in our day that no single author can present in a few pages even the most exhilarating discoveries that may be of help to us.

For Further Discussion

1. How can we discuss life's basic issues in small groups, as informally as possible? Why does this prove awkward at times? How did Christ deal with Zacchaeus? With Matthew?

2. What is Paul Tillich trying to tell us in these statements: "Man is the question, not the answer," or when he asserts that if there is no question to which revelation is the answer, "the revelatory answer is meaningless"? [3]

3. Luther suggested that an evangelical theology must begin "not from above but from below." Did he practice this approach?

4. What assertion in our traditional theology confronts you with agonizing problems? Which problems seem peripheral?

5. The Bible contains many accounts of calling, very few of conversion. All we can do in the power of the Spirit is to confront men with legitimate options. To delineate these clearly, to present alternatives which are basic and not peripheral, to avoid answers to some questions, and not to answer too many, is our greatest privilege and burden. When do these pages and our discussion fail in this and when do we succeed?

6. What is this author trying to say? "I take it that the doctrine of the Virgin Birth was formulated in order to preserve the truth of a real Incarnation by God. Now it is conceivable that, as a result of our modern understanding of genetics, it might be necessary to believe in the natural conception of Jesus for precisely the same reason, in order to preserve a doctrine of true Incarnation by God." [4]

7. If there are some statements in the Bible which are contradictory, then what assurance have we that others are valid?

8. Contemporary theology is like the waves of the sea, but the sea remains. The waves can upset a boat, but the ocean endures. Can this be said of all our theology? What is the difference between theology and faith?

9. Do you agree with the former general secretary of the World Council of Churches when he underscored the estrangement between the generations today and described it as: "the tension between the younger generation which takes nothing for granted, which does not trust any established values and institutions, and an older generation which seeks to defend, often without conviction or good reasons, these values and institutions. . . . Are we ready to distinguish between that which must be defended because it belongs to the essence of Christian truth and that which belongs only to the established status quo?" [5]

10. "The institutional church seems to the outsider to be more like a feudal society or a paternalistic family structure than a vital and free people of God." [6] Why do statements such as this arise from within the church?

11. What are these two young people saying, both from church-oriented backgrounds? "Around 10th grade in high school I started wondering about Christianity, wondering if all this they were feeding me for all these years wasn't a bunch of bull. I seriously questioned for a few years, but I was president of my church group through my junior year in high school, and I went through all the motions. I was actually the epitome of hypocrisy. But I finally came to the decision that I couldn't find any meaning in Christianity. I read a good deal of Camus and Kierkegaard, and I got hung up on some kind of existential philosophy, seeing that no broad dogma could be adhered to by everyone and that each person has to find his own truth. This is part of my alienation now. I'm sort of withdrawing philosophically and religiously from the established religion, and I'm trying to grapple with myself and find some philosophy to suit my own needs." [7]

12. "We all know the race crisis, about poverty, about blundering foreign policies, about the vast wasteland that pretends to be higher education, about the poverty of quality and style that marks the average American life and the joke that passes itself off as the gathering of the followers of Jesus Christ. . . . For the Christian of this new generation there is no enemy, certainly no ideological enemy in terms of competitive economic and philosophic systems. There are only brothers whom we are called to love and serve for Christ's sake." [8]

13. What did he mean? When Ignatius, Bishop of Antioch, was

thrown to lions (about 100 A.D.) he wrote shortly before his death: "Fire, cross and fighting with beasts, laceration, tearing apart, breaking of bones, wrenching of limbs, shattering of the whole body, cruel torments from the devil—all may come upon me, if only I may go to Jesus Christ. . . . Allow me to receive the pure light; once I have reached that point, I shall be a man."

14. Why are prophets usually persecuted?

15. We are clearly influenced by geography. Americans find it difficult to distinguish between faith and works. Europeans seem unable to differentiate between faith and theology. How did even your particular family background color your religious convictions?

16. Is it possible to discuss the things a Christian ought to believe in such a way as to avoid the issue of faith? "In the same degree that you direct attention to the definite things a man must believe, in that same degree do you get away from faith." [9]

17. Is frequency of church attendance a barometer of faith?

18. Where do we start in religion? Referring to the change in approach a popular theologian suggests: "Is it possible for Christians to accept this shift in the entire frame of reference—and not sell out? This, I believe, is a very big question, the biggest question for the future of Christianity in our day. . . . I am *not* suggesting an abandonment of the Christian gospel nor a substitution for it of a pure humanism. Neither am I proposing simply to turn my back on a theology of revelation and replace it with a 'natural theology' which begins with the presuppositions of human nature and hopes to arrive at Christianity from them. That would be to go back on all my generation in theology has learned." [10]

19. According to the incarnational principle those engaged in evangelistic effort identify themselves fully with those they want to influence. Is this the approach we are accustomed to? What does the expression "socratic evangelism" say to you?

20. The purpose of Christian education and of our study here is to confront men with legitimate options or "to answer the questions people have and then to lead them to ask such questions as only the Gospel can answer." Can we share some of our basic concerns? Does the Gospel offer any help in these areas?

Books for Suggested Reading

1. Mark Gibbs and T. R. Morton, *God's Frozen People*. Westminster, 1965.

2. William Stringfellow, *A Private or a Public Faith*. Eerdmans, 1962.

3. John H. Griffin, *Black Like Me*. New American Library, 1961.

4. Martin Marty, *The New Shape of American Religion*. Harper, 1959.

5. J. A. T. Robinson, *Honest to God*. Westminster, 1963.

6. Viktor E. Frankl, *Man's Search for Meaning*. Beacon, 1959.

7. Colin Williams, *Faith in a Secular Age*. Harper, 1966.

8. Jean-Paul Sartre, *No Exit*. Knopf, 1947.

CHAPTER THREE

WHO HAS THE LANTERN?

This I know: I am a human being. We may come from many different backgrounds, but we have one thing in common—we all participate in human existence. This is a universal answer but not a simple one. For when we ask, "What makes one truly human?" the answers become more varied and shadowy. Aristotle maintains that the only difference between man and animal is that man cooks his food. We can still view man from many other aspects. To the medic I am flesh and blood; to the chemist I am a compound of substances; to the psychiatrist, a bundle of nerves; to the philosopher, a subject of study; to the post office, an address; to the politician, a voter; to the government, a taxpayer. History can be of some help, for history is simply the study of man. Christian history is the study of man's relationship to God.

The Christian faith, also, is struggling with this question today as never before and asks primarily: Who am I before God? What is my relationship to him? Why was I created in the first place?

Answers a great theologian: "The basic phenomenon peculiar to man is the consciousness of responsibility."[1]

Or it can be said that for Christianity what is fundamentally human in human nature is the gift to man of the power to be and to fulfill himself in and through a relationship of dependence and self-giving toward God and toward his fellow man. Expressed more simply, I am not really and fully a human being unless I am properly related to God and to others.

Of course, I may prefer not to be fully human. I may prefer

16

to live on the level of an animal. The older distinction that man
has a mind and/or a soul while the animal species does not is
hardly valid today, or at least it is rather meaningless. If man is
a self-conscious center of action, then I should be fully conscious
of my actions.

"Before one seeks for man, one must have found the Lantern."
"Bevor man den Menschen sucht, muss man die Laterne gefunden
haben" (Nietzsche, *Menschliches, Allzumenschliches*, II, 7).

Who has the Lantern? The scientist does not claim to be able
to discover man's ultimate meaning or purpose, for he explains
all phenomena, all occurrences, on the basis of natural causes.
He is aware of the marvelous fact that nature is unified and
operates according to laws and not by whims or chaos.

But this is not the total picture. And few scientists go out of
their domain to assert that life is nothing but a chemical process;
the world is nothing but a machine; life is nothing more than
genes and chromosomes.

The question of man remains; sometimes it haunts us, at other
times we try hard to ignore it. But it is to this question, Christians
believe, that God has directed himself. And while men have
often become embroiled in debates about the evolutionary process or the chronology of beginnings—a study for scientists—it
is for us to determine what God says about us.

The Right Man

Sometimes the best approach is to begin our search with The
Man, Jesus Christ. Here was one who personified everything that
is truly human in his relationship to God and to his fellow human
beings. He was concerned with ultimate issues, even with eternity, but never at the expense of turning a deaf ear to others who
needed him. He was aware of changing conditions which confronted his generation and dared to oppose the power structures
of his day which clearly had dehumanized man. He did not subject himself blindly to what the religious leaders of his day
preached but questioned their authority and their doctrines. He
was not even afraid of doubt and even came close to despair
himself in the Garden of Gethsemane and on the cross. He was
aware of man's predicament and was kept busy healing and

helping until his own health was being ruined. He spent more time and effort in talking to God rather than merely talking about him. He gave his life to reconcile people to each other and to God. His acts were as important as his words, but he spoke much about faith.

If one were to read for the first time the original record of him, usually called the Gospel of Mark, what would one find? Something like this:

A young Jew, filled with God's Spirit, did strange and powerful deeds, helping and healing those who were in the grip of evil. He also spoke exceptionally powerful words. At the instigation of his contemporaries he was cruelly put to death. But God raised him again from the grave. This was all in accord with what God had outlined in the Jewish Scriptures. Because of what happened some maintained that Jesus was God's supreme agent for the rescue of mankind and, in fact, for the fulfillment of his purpose in the entire world. All who hear this are confronted with the challenge to trust him, to be baptized in his name, and to proclaim this good news to others by helping them as he did.

Many of the details about his life and death and words are blurred, but this can be said without equivocation: He had a high estimate of man. Brilliant and gifted, he could have spent his time in metaphysical discussions at the university, but he was too busy helping others. His knowledge of man has never been excelled. The following could be delineated as the major thrusts of his conception of man, especially as he inherited these from the Jewish Scriptures.

Addressable

Man is addressable by God. Whether Adam was an individual or a crowd, this stands out in the scriptural account of creation: God spoke to Adam and Eve. He did not address the animals or the stars. Some of the details in Genesis may sound primitive to us, but we cannot escape this discovery, namely that in some way God always impinges upon our lives.

Whether this fact was always seen clearly in the past is not our concern now. But few would deny that since man is addressable by God he cannot avoid what is usually described as "confrontation." To live is to be confronted. Our problem then is probably not that we cannot "find God," but that we try to escape confrontation with God.

Responsible

Not only did God address Adam and Eve—he also held them responsible for their words and their actions. As far as we know, he did not approach any other living forms in this way.

Sometimes men have argued about the "how" of man's origin or even arrayed arguments for or against theories of evolution in an attempt to evade this confrontation of responsibility. Darrow and Bryan in their famous encounter might have served men better had they devoted their energy and gifts to assisting others rather than engaging in a fruitless argument and running away from basic issues.

If we are made in "the image of God," it may well be that a major aspect of this is the fact that we are addressable by God and responsible to him. The "search for identity," a genuine problem in our day, may well be a search for God. Man cannot not be man, but in his estrangement he tries to evade the choice of obeying or disobeying God. Chapters 1 and 3 of Genesis give us the true picture of man, though this is not how man usually pictures himself in relation to God. Man claims that God is a problem to him, but Genesis reminds us that man's problem is that he tries to flee from a God from whom one cannot flee.

Helpless

Christ seemed to be convinced of another truth about man— namely, that man needs help, for Jesus went about doing good— helping, healing, counseling, instructing.

We can use a dozen different metaphors in an attempt to describe this condition of man. Poets may underscore "the tragic view of man," painters may try to depict man's inhumanity to man, counselors cannot escape the fact of man's alienation from man.

The whole emphasis may be somewhat depressing, yet it is realistic. No one, exactly no one—even with the best of efforts— always loves everyone or acts consistently from the purest of motives. Innately, man is a rebel—unlovely, unkind, selfish.

According to Christ, our basic problem is that we ought to love God and our neighbor as ourselves—yet we cannot respond as we ought. What is unique in Christ's estimate of man is not that we are estranged and alienated but that the source of all this rests in our relationship to God. Adam and Eve insisted on gaining knowledge that belongs only to God. The Israelites trusted the golden calf rather than God; they preferred a king to God; they trusted Egypt and other nations rather than God. An excellent illustration from the New Testament is the parable of the rich fool, the portrayal of a man who placed his ultimate loyalty in his material possessions rather than in God (Luke 12:16-21).

Traditionally this helplessness of man has been traced to the sin of pride or unbelief. Nothing that man does is free from unbelief (Romans 3:23) and there is no one exempt from this (Romans 3:10). We can smooth over this truth or take tranquilizers to forget it, but that does not remove it. Sometimes it's like a bad dream—you stand there naked, unable to help yourself.

History and Man

The fourth major disclosure of Jesus about man is encouraging, for he was convinced that man could change, that he could be helped, that he could recover from his estrangement and alienation. The only alternative is total despair.

According to Christ's own statements, this is the major reason why he came and lived and died and arose: his high estimate of man. The first hint of this is given early in the history of man (Genesis 3:15). From then on God's approach to man is a long and involved story, but it is focused on the appearance of Christ. In fact, the entire cosmos exists to make Bethlehem possible. History and man now are given meaning and purpose. Not all problems have been solved, but now man has been given a reason for existence, and our ultimate purpose is to be truly human.

For Further Discussion

1. In your words, what makes us truly human? Does Psalm 8 help?

2. What is nihilism?

3. What is meant by "genetic programming"? Is this an attempt by man to play God, or is this a way of subduing the earth? Does science have an ethic?

4. Why does religious faith make such a sharp distinction between an observer and a participant?

5. "An illustration of ineffective ministry resulting from ignorance of actual need is the widespread use of charity as a cure-all for slum conditions. It is known in the black ghettos as 'plantation charity.' . . . It is a variation of the old established 'Christmas basket charity' so often practiced by Christians, with the only difference being that instead of occurring once a year along with the holiday spirit, plantation charity lasts 365 days a year. Based on an assumption that people in need are inferior to the person giving aid, plantation charity is the most foolish and most despised of all efforts to minister to poverty-stricken people. Such a relationship . . . classifies the recipients as helpless people who are solely responsible for their sorrowful condition. The beneficiary of such charity is the giver. . . . His responsibility, as a part of the society that has created the slum ghetto and used charity as a means of sustaining it, is overshadowed by his feeling of goodness."[2]

6. Have you ever meditated on Chapter 28 of the Book of Job? Does Job believe in deism, according to which the world is a machine started by a watchmaker God? Does he believe in pantheism, where God cannot be separated from the world he created? Does he believe that evil rules the world?

7. On the fiftieth anniversary of Communism in Russia prominent posters declared: "We will never be forgotten . . . we have given substance to the word 'man.'" Communism has certainly spread in the last half century. Why?

8. How does Christianity differ from humanistic ideologies?

9. What is the difference between disbelief and unbelief?

10. Does modern man worry about his sin? Is there a basic sin such as pride or sloth?

11. What scriptural passages, in addition to Genesis 1, speak of man as created by God?

12. Some contemporary writers, often in a deceptively simple

way, depict man's simultaneous rise and fall, buttressing the Christian view that original sin is an anthropological fact. One of them likes to describe men as "trying to clean out their guts"; another pictures children who end up murdering one another. What modern literary work says much the same to you?

13. Most people are born originals, but they die as copies. Does this statement make you smile or cry?

14. "I feel sorry for theologians. They are lonely. So am I."[3]

15. For those who can discuss with intensity: "For Christianity, what is fundamentally human in human nature is the gift to man of the power to be and to fulfill himself in and through a relationship of dependence and self-giving toward God and toward his fellow man. Thus, maturity is self-acceptance through self-giving."[4]

16. Jesus loved good food, and Paul suggested drinking some wine. How about some coffee and cookies during our discussion? Should this discussion be a satisfying and even a happy experience?

17. "Every time theology intrudes into the domain of science, it will inexorably end up defeated. This is not one of the least important aspects of the return to what is basic: faith can only be itself if it completely abandons the ground of science."[5] How do you square this with the assertion that our Christian faith is to be concerned with all of life? How would you answer the surgeon who said, "I found no soul at the end of my scalpel"?

18. Science can study man from countless aspects. But why does man exist? Give an illustration of a false struggle between science and religion. Does faith have a different kind of certainty than science? How does the Christian faith solve the mystery of existence?

19. Which do we need more, the psychologist's or philosopher's discovery of man's anxiety, guilt, and estrangement, or the Christian Gospel's solution to modern man's predicament? Do you know of anyone who has found the solution? Would a solution involve all of life—including farming, the stock market, the pill?

20. Christ is love, and love overcomes divisions. In Christ I

can be my real self and live for others. Only contact with the New Being, Jesus Christ, can overcome conflicts in our existence. If the psychiatrist or the doctor participates in healing, then he becomes an instrument of Christ's grace. Even if he is an unbeliever?

21. Maturity is self-acceptance through self-giving. How did we say this in traditional phrases?

22. Christ is the one "in whom all things hold together." Does this refer to individuals? How does this presuppose the brokenness of man as well as man's need and capacity for forgiveness and reconciliation?

23. The last two lines of Johann Sebastian Bach's Christmas Oratorio state, "Bei Gott hat seine Stelle Das menschliche Geschlecht." Could this be said also of the other festivals?

24. At a time when the church supported slavery, failed to distribute food, and catered to the rich, Karl Marx wrote, "Religion is the sigh of creation in torment, the soul of a heartless world, a mentality formed on mindless objects. It is the opium of the people." Did he see the true church?

25. In the genealogy of Jesus why does Matthew mention only four women, all Gentiles: Tamar, Rahab, Ruth, and Bathsheba?

26. Do the following say anything about the incarnation: the angel Gabriel's announcement in the Book of Daniel, Exodus 40:34-35, 2 Chronicles 7:2?

27. The miracles say over and over again: Jesus helps.

28. Should parents force a fifteen-year-old to go to church?

29. What particular talents do you place in the service of man and hence of God?

30. "The Christian is simply a man who is in the process of being restored to his normal human manhood."[6]

31. "Man did not descend from the ape, he ascended."[7]

32. Never in history has a society treated its poor so poorly. On an average eighty people are bitten by rats every month in East Harlem. Are these problems on God's agenda? (Isaiah 58:1-6.)

Books for Suggested Reading

1. Erik Routley, *The Man for Others.* Oxford University Press, 1964.

2. Roger Hazelton, *Christ and Ourselves.* Harper, 1965.

3. Kent S. Knutson, *His Only Son Our Lord.* Augsburg, 1966.

4. Clarence King, *Working with People in Community Action.* Association, 1965.

5. C. Ellis Nelson, *Where Faith Begins.* John Knox, 1967.

6. Erich Fromm, *Man for Himself.* Holt, Rinehart, 1942.

7. Walther Eichrodt, *Man in the Old Testament.* Allenson, 1956.

8. Martin Luther, *On the Bondage of the Will,* tr. J. I. Packer and O. R. Johnston. Fleming H. Revell Co. 1957.

CHAPTER FOUR

GOD

We have been engaging in a good deal of God-talk, simply assuming there is a God.

What if there is no God?

This question is one of the two major problems in our religious life today. The other concerns the church—even if there is a God, even if Christ is authentic, has not the church betrayed him?

One of the difficulties in speaking of God is that the term has become almost meaningless. What do you refer to when you say "God"? Is he the grand architect of the universe, man's ultimate concern, the ground of being, a person, a voice? Jesus suggested that we call him "Daddy" (abba). That may be a lovely suggestion, but how can I? Does anyone else feel that close to him?

No one has a full and clear and complete answer to the question: "What is God like?" If he did, he would not be speaking about "God." Sometimes we become positively nauseated by people who think that they can speak for God, as if they could look over his shoulder and anticipate his next move. How can anyone assert that God wants us to engage in war, that God blesses a certain marriage, that God thinks we ought to build elaborate church buildings while thousands of human beings are starving?

Ways of Escape

There are several ways of escape. We may try to return to the "good old days" when few questioned the existence of God. This, however, is impossible. We simply cannot return to the Middle Ages.

Or we can evade him by engaging in a "flight to religiosity," becoming extremely busy doing acts of charity, praying, and reading the Bible. At such times we may urge others on by throwing about such clichés as, "You ought to do the will of God," when no one knows what the will of God is in this particular situation. Personal confrontation suggests a yes or no alternative, and a long time ago someone suggested that anything which goes beyond this "yea and nay" is of the devil.

How does one define confrontation with ultimate mystery? We should be aware of the fact that "to form an image of God or His acts is to deny His existence." [1] One can make graven images of God even on a piece of paper, for "Who can understand his ways?"

And yet, God is there. I may agree at times with Albert Camus when he sighs, "I should like to be a saint but without God." Yet I can't, not only can I not be a saint, I cannot even be human without God. One begins to sense why we are told that "Moses entered into the thick darkness where God was."

It may help us to begin negatively. Those of us who were brought up in a Christian environment have learned to speak of God as a "person." Unfortunately this term no longer carries the same freight as it once did, for we have been so oriented psychologically as to think of a personality. But God is not just "someone." If we think of him as "someone," only one aspect of him meets us, and a very limited aspect at that; as if God were one among a group of others, albeit the greatest of them all.

"If I see the matter correctly, the crisis of the idea of God since the eighteenth century is connected chiefly with the problem of how the power determinative of all reality can be conceived of as a person." [2]

The Cry of Centuries

In this dilemma we should listen to contemporary attempts in the search for God, though in many ways these echo the cry of centuries.

Whether we use the word "person" of God is not essential. Yet he acts—in creation, by sending wind and rain, storm, and food. Even that does not help us much.

Ultimately I am driven to approach God through one who

made any kind of approach possible for us. When I think of God I think of Christ. Even here there is endless mystery, but at least I can speak to him and identify with him. And it may happen that sometimes I find it difficult to converse with him, yet simply appreciate his presence without the sound of words while my being is attuned to him, for he is more than man—he comes to me from all sides, from above, below, and within and without.

The moment we suggest, however, that God can be approached—though never fully understood—in Jesus Christ, we are confronted immediately by the second great stumbling-block as far as the Christian God is concerned.

Why do Christians speak of three persons? Originally, the word *persona* in classical Latin designated a mask which an actor wore as he played a particular role on the stage. Is God, then, playing three particular roles as Father, Son, and Holy Spirit? This, again, is an oversimplification, for there is nothing "phony" about God. Hence the suggestion has been made, and I know of none better, that we speak of God in three realities, lest we separate him into three Gods. In the first century a "person" was a free citizen, hence a slave was not considered a person. In Christ we are all persons—everyone is of value, even the cripple and the retarded and the homosexual. Merely to repeat ancient statements may not only not contribute to our lives today but may even hinder true faith. The greater the historical and cultural interval between an event or a document and the reader, the more difficult the explanation becomes. I can, of course, sing: "I should like to have been with him then" and thereby indicate that I cannot be with him now.

A Useless Search

Some of us may as well admit that most of our lives we have had three Gods. We speak of the Creator or the Father and ignore the Son, or we speak of Christ and hardly ever mention the Holy Spirit. I can evade confrontation with God by discussing the trinitarian aspects of his deity.

This may have to be established first: We know nothing about God unless he tells us about himself. Unless he chooses to do so, our search is absolutely useless.

In a way, of course, God has revealed himself in nature and in man. Technically, we had better call this a kind of self-disclosure of God in nature. From it we can ascertain that God is powerful, majestic, and, in a way, wise. But this kind of deduction is not very helpful, for this God also permits earthquakes that swallow whole cities and famines that starve thousands. The sociologist who studies the family, or the economist and the politician are all in a way trying to decipher what planning and ordering and laws are a part of this creation. How fascinating and positively scintillating such efforts can be is becoming increasingly apparent.

But this general self-disclosure of God in nature is not particularly satisfying, especially as we are confronted by the suffering of man. When we stand at the deathbed of a child, or see pictures of man's inhumanity to man, the latest discoveries of science in splitting the atom seem a bit tasteless.

These Last Days

Through the centuries many have come to the conviction that in addition to God's vague self-disclosure in nature he has revealed himself much more specifically in Jesus Christ. Early believers put it this way, "In many and various ways God spoke of old to our fathers by the prophets; but in these last days he has spoken to us by a Son" (Hebrews 1:1).

In a way this "leap of faith" presents as many problems as it solves. For now we have to believe that God has revealed himself to man and that this has been correctly recorded in the Bible—else how would we know what he said and did?

According to the Christian view, God revealed himself most clearly in Jesus Christ. One of the grandest truths revealed by Christ is that we do not have to know everything there is to know about him. His primary concern was not that we engage in intellectual feats about him—speaking in involved terms about his two natures, inseparable and indivisible, and whether he wore the robe of a rabbi or the clothes of a carpenter—but that we are helped by what he did for us.

In fact, knowing about Christ and God is not the ultimate concern at all. This is a necessary preliminary stage, but in the end what counts is what he has done for us and whether he can give any meaning to our lives. No one knows the exact day when he was born, for not until the sixth century did men begin to count years (B.C. and A.D.) from the time of Jesus' birth, or when he died on the cross. Nor do we know whether his ministry lasted for two or three years.

But this we do know: He was concerned with people, he addressed men in their actual situation, and he loved others to the bitter end.

Our relationship to this God is a matter of faith, for faith is primarily relationship. "The Christian's act of faith cannot consist in assenting to the proposition 'I believe in God'; though he cannot very well have Christian faith without actually conceptualizing his belief (and, therefore, expressing it, at least to himself) in some such proposition as 'I believe in God.' But belief must bear directly upon the reality of God, not upon words or upon concepts . . . . It may be that saying about God all we can, but being also as silent as we can regarding his name, might increase the meaningfulness of whatever religious experience we may wish to convey to others, to ourselves and to God." [3]

For Further Discussion

1. "The man of today no longer asks, 'How can I find a gracious God?' His question is more radical, more elementary; he asks about God as such, 'Where is God?' He suffers not from God's wrath, but from the impression of his absence; he asks not about a gracious God, but whether God really exists." [4]

2. The expression "flight to religiosity" comes from Rudolf Bultmann. For further information consult: Walter Schmithals *Introduction to the Theology of Rudolf Bultmann,* tr. John Bowden (Augsburg, 1968).

3. What is your favorite way of escaping God? I think mine is by studying religious articles and writing lectures and books about him.

4. "Strict orthodoxy is as much the result of mutual suspicion as of ardent faith." [5]

5. Would you agree that the easiest place to avoid God is in a church building? Can one be justified by faith in an institution?

6. "The highest bondage knows no pressure" (Martin Buber). In what way have you experienced this? How do you react to another statement of his: "He who decides with all his soul decides for God"?

7. If politics is an attempt to keep human life human, is God a politician?

8. Paul Tillich has said that there is no truth without doubt, no doubt without truth. He speaks of the artist as the priest of the future church.[6] Why is art so important to religion? "The road beyond psychology leads to a point where art and religion meet, join, and transform each other." [7]

9. One of our greatest minds had to admit, "I do not know how it is possible to believe in anything pertaining to God and eternity 'literally.' " [8]

10. Would it be an improvement if our worship services were begun, "In the Name of God" rather than, "In the Name of the Father, and of the Son, and of the Holy Spirit"? How, then, could the concept of Trinity be added?

11. Do you know of any groups who seem to be guilty of a unitarianism of one person in the Trinity? Where do we stand?

12. Does the distinction between law and gospel, so dear to theologians, have any meaning for you? If so, how? Would someone in the group present a brief resumé of this emphasis in ordinary language next time? Can the law be compared to Mary and the gospel to Jesus Christ?

13. Would a "learning pill" help us become better Christians?

14. Which is more important: to discuss whether God is dead or to help God be God, not in himself but in us?

15. Why does the church engage in so much double-talk about God? Everything comes from him, but not evil. He loves everyone and yet damns some. Which one can you add?

16. If God has the whole world in his hands, what about the thousands who starved to death yesterday?

17. Graham Greene maintained that he would refuse to believe in a God whom he could understand. St. Teresa of Avila thanked God that there was much in the Bible she could not understand. Do these say anything to you about God? 1 Timothy 6:16, Acts 17:28, Genesis 2:7, Hebrews 12:29, Psalm 3:4, Luke 15:20.

18. In "Something About Believing," Duke Ellington and his singers seem to offer a spirited rejection of the "God Is Dead" cliché when they declaim at one point,

> The mere mention of the first word
> Au - to - mat - i - cal - ly e - lim - in - ates
> The second and the third.

19. God reveals *himself*, not words or concepts or doctrines about himself. The response he desires is that of faith in him. There's a world of difference between speaking about him and believing in him.

20. Do you agree?

a. The image of God in man is his creation for life in community.

b. Your neighbor becomes more important to you because you believe in Christ.

c. The Trinity helps to keep God from becoming an absolute monarch.

d. Most of my life I have spent trying to run away from God.

e. Atheism is not new but what is new is that even in the church God has become a problem.

f. "I believe in God" is man's ultimate assertion.

g. Faith is a relationship.

h. Matthew 25:40.

21. Cyril C. Richardson calls the doctrine of the Trinity "an artificial construct" because of the imposition of "threeness." [9]

22. In moments of mortal danger God seems near. Why not now?

23. How can the following statements be helpful to us?

a. "Immediacy should follow reflection"—Søren Kierkegaard.

b. "God is not expressible, only addressable"—Martin Buber.

c. Faith applies to all of life, for when you say "you" to God everything else becomes subordinate.

d. "The most difficult word in the Bible is the word 'your' in 'I am the Lord your God'"—Martin Luther.

e. "Religious thinking is in perpetual danger of giving primacy to concepts and dogmas and to forfeit the immediacy of insights, to forget that the known is but a reminder of God, that the dogma is a token of His will, the expression the inexpressible at its minimum. Concepts, words must not become screens; they must be regarded as windows. . . . The roots of ultimate insights are found . . . not on the level of discursive thinking, but on the level of wonder and radical amazement, in the depth of awe, in our sensitivity to the mystery, in our awareness of the ineffable." [10]

24. Would recent studies indicate that more of the Bible is liturgy and hymns than we formerly believed? Dr. Krister Stendahl refers to the religious language of the Bible as "poetry-plus rather than science-minus."

25. Would it be better not to have pictures of God, only of what he does?

26. "Occasionally it is even easier to recognize Christ in the world than in the church." [11] Why is this said with such frequency?

27. Is it better to speak of a church building as God's house or the house of God's people?

28. When Thomas said "My Lord and my God," was that faith or theology?

29. "The basic theological problem today is the reality of God" (Langdon Gilkey). How does this statement differ from that of Dietrich Bonhoeffer: "We are proceeding toward a time of no religion at all"? What do these statements say to the nearly one of every two people on earth who live in the thralldom of totalitarian governments which condemn religion as the opiate of the masses?

How does this differ from the "atheism of distraction" which says, "I'm just too busy to think about God at all"?

30. Is this a common experience: People who lash out against the times in which they live are liable to make one of two mistakes. They may blame the contemporary situation for evils which have been fairly constant throughout history and perhaps are inherent in the human situation. Or they universalize their personal problems. This is not an easy day in which to believe in God, but it is even harder not to believe in him.

31. What do the prophets mean when they excoriate the chosen people for whoring after strange gods? Who decides which gods are strange? If God is unknowable, why try to prove his existence?

32. Are these viable options?
a. Stop talking about God.
b. Simply repeat biblical statements.
c. Formulate a new image and concept of God, using contemporary thought categories.
d. Assist in expressing the presence of "the man for others."

33. How do they differ: the Pharisee who knew his Bible, and the worried father who pleaded, "I believe; help my unbelief"?

34. "For all the unwarranted and inexpedient inadequacies of the Christian faith today, and for all the underdevelopment of its theism, what is most typical of the present moment of Christianity is not that it suffers from these, by now inveterate inadequacies, but that the suffering has become acutely painful and threatens to become unbearable. This is the sign of fundamental health at the core of the Church. It reveals a heightening of self-consciousness, and where there is self-consciousness there is hope. The need for proper medication is fairly commonly avowed." [12]

35. Usually writings on God are of two kinds. Some contribute to ideas on theology, often taking sides and offering solutions. Others offer devotional assistance and seek to encourage faith and loyalty. Should these two ever be separated? Do these pages instruct or inspire? Which do we need most?

Books for Suggested Reading

1. Robert Marshall, *The Mighty Acts of God.* Lutheran Church Press, 1964.

2. Helmut Thielicke, *The Waiting Father,* tr. John W. Doberstein. Harper, 1959.

3. Karl Rahner, *Encounter with Silence,* tr. James Demske. Newman, 1964.

4. G. Ernest Wright, *God Who Acts.* SCM, 1952.

5. Claude Welch, *In His Name.* Scribner, 1952.

6. Roger Hazelton, *A Theological Approach to Art.* Abingdon, 1967.

7. Cyril C. Richardson, *The Doctrine of the Trinity.* Abingdon, 1958.

8. Martin Buber, *On Judaism,* edited by Nahum N. Glatzer. Schocken, 1967.

9. Leslie Dewart, *The Future of Belief.* Herder and Herder, 1967.

CHAPTER FIVE

PLANNED HISTORY

Christ viewed himself as a part of history.

"The hour is come," he said on the last evening of his life. What hour? Centuries upon centuries of planned history had led up to this hour. Here is the hinge on which all history turns.

When was this plan begun? No one knows, for it literally originated in the heart of God. Out of pure, unexpurgated, uncaused love *(agape)* he decided to create man and to take care of him. Even when man revolted against God by trying to become something more than a human being God was still concerned with his welfare. That our whole existence is marred by guilt and death is dramatically pictured in Job 30:17-30 and 14:18-20. Fortunately the Christian faith does not claim to solve all mysteries of existence.

To avoid attributing to God our own ambiguous fantasies is extremely difficult. In controversial areas it is better to leave many problems unsolved, rather than to supply traditional though unsatisfactory answers in the hope that even the little we have been given will help us face reality with candor and honesty.

A Case Study

Not all that God did and said has been recorded for us. But if Christ saw himself as the culmination of God's plan, it may help us to delve briefly into the background of Christ, to make

35

a "case study" as it were, so that our decision concerning him be
as responsible as possible. In this attempt we ought to be conscious constantly that language not become the barrier of experience. Not the terms used—which can always be debated—but the
vision of reality is important. The meaning of a sentence as it
impresses the reader is important but the meaning of the sen-
tence-maker is more important.

How and when God created man we do not know. When in
the dim past an "it" first becomes a "who" we cannot tell. When
men first rebelled against their Creator is also veiled in mystery.

But then came a moment when, after centuries of wandering
and propagating and suffering, one man was chosen by God for
a very special purpose. About 1500 B.C. in a mysterious manner
God took hold of Abraham, not because he was better than
others but because God had decided to choose him, and through
him inaugurated a special plan to help mankind. Abraham
turned out to be a man of faith who trusted God with a kind of
sanctified stubbornness. Through his children and grandchildren
he became the father of a distinct nation usually referred to as
Israelites or Jews or the Chosen Nation.

We probably recall how after a time a famine forced them to
go to Egypt for food and how centuries later they were led out
again by one of history's greatest, Moses. Through him God—
or Yahweh, as they called him—revealed that there is only one
God (monotheism), that he is unique and different from all
creatures, and that he is a God who loves us. In some ways this
was the grandest revelation in the Old Testament. Through
Moses mankind also received the Commandments.

The history of this people becomes quite involved, for God sent
judges, such as Samson and Gideon, to remind them of their
responsibility to God. There were savage periods in their history when they butchered and killed and massacred just as we do
today. After they had entered the land of Canaan they remained
true to their God Yahweh instead of adopting the gods of the
land, as conquerors often did.

If it was a gift of revelation that God is one, then it is also
worthy of note that when the children of Israel occupied the
promised land and ceased their nomadic wanderings they maintained their ancestral God—a God who governed more than

We Have a Dream

Freedom demonstrators
in Selma, Alabama.

Photo: Religious News Service.

Follow Me

Crucifix by Philip Thompson.

*Photo courtesy of Lutheran Society
for Worship, Music and the Arts.*

**Created Free
and Equal**

Creation relief sculpture
by Robert Aldern.

*Photo courtesy of Lutheran Society
for Worship, Music and the Arts.*

Until All Men Are Free

The Crucifixion by Paul Granlund.

*Photo courtesy of Lutheran Society
for Worship, Music and the Arts.*

their few acres. Their God belonged not only to a glorious past but was also always leading toward a better future.

In fact, their entire history is unusually strange, because God was forging out his plans. Sometime later these people under King David conquered Jerusalem and made it their capital so they could be a full-fledged political kingdom. Yet they did not worship the king as other nations did but retained their faith in Yahweh. When they often weakened and fell for pagan gods Yahweh would send them prophets to remind them of their reason for existence and of their responsibility to God. Always there seemed to be a remnant of faithful people around ready to respond, through whom the whole nation was renewed again and again.

A Unique Revelation

Later on, when arguments and wars split them, the people of the Southern Kingdom were transported as a group to Babylon. In this way their unique revelation or religion was saved, for here in a strange environment they experienced anew that Yahweh was their God. Through prophets like Isaiah they were reminded that their God is a gracious God who is concerned about people and who is eager to help, especially through the sending of a Messiah.

Because of a change in the political situation about 500 B.C. many of these Jews returned to rebuild their beloved Jerusalem.

Here is a concentration of history as planned by God. It included many men and women of simple, deep, and influential faith. Some of their acts and words have been an inspiration to mankind through the centuries. That God was also active through the history of other nations seems to be beyond doubt, for he is a God of all.[1]

What did all this mean? Lest all these complicated strains of Israel's history be lost in details, God sent explanations, mostly through the prophets. Since prophets were sometimes honored, false ones also arose who appealed to their contemporaries by assuring them that everything was going according to God's will; the common people often found it difficult to distinguish between the real prophets and the phonies. Sometimes even kings tried to change the messages of authentic prophets. But by

God's mysterious leading the truth was passed on, usually through liturgy and songs and psalms and stories retold around the family circle.

Sacred Writings

A few words began to stand out in this tradition: covenant, justice, Messiah, lovingkindness, sin, sacrifice, Spirit, law, marriage, mercy, peace, wisdom. These words began to acquire meanings peculiar to this nation. They spoke much of their history—what Yahweh had done here and there—for they were convinced that God was active here in this world and that the centuries were leading up to something worth while.

All this history was so important that about the time of the exile they began to collect sayings and songs as they had been passed on by oral tradition. As more and more were collected and written down, the books now known as the Old Testament became very precious to them, for here they encountered God over and over again and were reminded that this God is to be worshiped. Their poets could go into ecstasies over these sacred books (see Deuteronomy 30:12-14, Isaiah 40:7-8). They became convinced that this word of the Lord would endure forever.

Not all that God had revealed to them was recorded, but evidently all that we need is preserved. The writing and the collecting were spread over almost a thousand years. Some books grew; the Psalms, for example, were gathered through the years. Scholars have spent long and weary hours trying to determine, by studying style and content, when each section was written and by whom. Some of this effort is valuable and important, for through it we can understand better God's ways with mankind. Often they recorded actual events, sometimes they interpreted their deeper meaning. Often they simply gushed over in their attempts because their God was so great and wonderful. Even dirty details are recorded—for that's the way man is. To get stuck on details or on questions like: "Did this actually happen under King So-and-so," may result in losing the real message, God's message to mankind.

For we dare not lose sight of the major thread in this vast array of details of prophets and prostitutes, of wars and intrigue, of songs and love—that all the while God in a mysterious way was

actively leading up to something important through the proc-
esses of history. That is why the Old Testament points so much
to the future with a heavy emphasis on how God's Spirit, who
caused the books to be written and gathered, was preparing his
people for the greatest moment in their history, the real reason
for their existence in God's plan. Isaiah, especially, had pointed
toward this fulfillment.

That moment came in Jesus Christ.

Briefly once more God prepared them for his coming through
the acts and words of John the Baptist. He was strongly judg-
mental, reminding his contemporaries that the moment of decision is to be faced not by engaging in a series of sacred acts
but in a change of heart, sometimes called conversion (Luke
3:10-14).

John soon recedes into the background so that the spotlight
can be fully focused on Christ.

We cannot begin to discuss everything that Christ said and
did, for this would require a lifetime and more. Certainly we are
not interested in reconstructing an exact biography, for this is
impossible on the basis of records we now have. While many of
the events—his birth, and death, and resurrection—actually happened, though we cannot date them precisely, it is not his ultimate
concern that we can repeat certain facts about him. The life of
Jesus is important, but the meaning of his life is much more
important. To engage here in an academic exercise is not difficult,
but to find ultimate answers in Christ is so basic that we need the
help of another. Jesus called him the Holy Spirit.

For Further Discussion

1. If God is love, why is there so much agony in the world?

2. Which aspect of the life of Christ is most meaningful to
you? Would you like to develop this for the whole group? Are
you acquainted with these exquisite short sayings of his—Matthew 5:15, 6:34; John 16:21; Luke 17:21?

3. What is the point of statements such as: History is the
coming into being of civilization, the successive and collective
effort which man as a social being has undertaken in order to
make the earth a suitable habitation. There is really only so-

cial history, for history encompasses the life of mankind. Revelation is formed in and through history. God is not man's competitor who can only win by causing his opponent to disappear.

4. What different kinds of love are there?

5. Dreams of incessant progress lie buried in battlefields and concentration camps and poverty-stricken ghettos. This may sound dismal, but this truth must question our presumed self-sufficiency. Is the Fall a valid symbol signifying man's situation as one of estrangement? How? Does a prophet proclaim doom or promise?

6. The moment, or *kairos*, can be defined as the moment God acts in or upon us, when we are faced with the responsibility to respond. There are many *kairoi*, all derived from the first one, the coming of Christ.

7. Among the choicest words in the Bible is *shalom* (peace)— a word which summarizes all the gifts of the messianic age. Even the name of the Messiah can simply be *shalom* (Micah 5:5, Ephesians 2:14). Our God is a god of *shalom* (Ephesians 6:15). *Shalom* is not something which we give—it is a social happening, an event in interpersonal relations.

8. Do you agree? The chief ground for optimism among Christians today is that many people have at last come to see the social implications of Christianity. Recent events and Bible study have helped to remove some of the cataracts from our eyes in that we can no longer seek a spiritual kingdom of God by turning our backs on the needs of men. We sense again the impact of Jesus' first sermon at Nazareth or his reaction to the rich young ruler. The four Gospels are not abstract ramblings about God but vivid accounts of how Christ lived, of his availability, the way he lifted the spirits of the poor, the way he dared the affluent to be concerned about others, the way he treated all as human beings. "He went about doing good."

9. What is the difference between viewing the Bible as a series of proof passages and considering it as normative authority for our faith?

10. Does it offend Jews that we call their Bible "old"?

11. The Bible must be read according to its own terms. Which of these is valid?

a. Salvation is the gift of freedom to be one's real self.

b. Flesh—as Paul uses this term—does not refer primarily to biological existence but to a way of life in which man boasts of his own security. It is an attempt to ground one's life in earthly securities which are disposable and controllable by man.

c. The spirituality of the legalist is as fleshly as that of the adulterer.

d. Hostility of the world refers to the temptation to serve things rather than people.

e. When we ask all to study the same portion of Scripture we are like the physician who gives everyone penicillin no matter what the ailment may be.

f. If we read a portion of the Bible each day, then God will bless us.

g. It is the world which provides the agenda for the church.

h. Worship springs out of and prepares one for involvement in the world.

i. Anything which makes us feel secure inside the walls of a holy place is heresy.

j. If we do not devise forms of worship which are of our day, we are denying the incarnation.

12. Some maintain that our basic problem today is one of hermeneutics. Hermeneutics may be defined as a study of the principles and methods of interpretation according to which the meaning of ancient texts is made accessible to contemporary understanding. The lamentable history of the conflict between science and religion is a monument to bad hermeneutics.

13. There are two kinds of stumbling-blocks which we encounter in the Bible—one legitimate, the other illegitimate. The wrong stumbling-block is erected by our inability to understand or communicate the Gospel effectively so that men can decide for or against the real thing. "What we have to do is to overcome the wrong stumbling-block in order to bring people face to face with the right stumbling-block and enable them to make a genuine decision." [2] Is this the same as removing the scandal or offense of the Gospel? Which episodes in the Book of Acts are helpful here?

14. Which Gospel excels in giving us the events in Jesus' life? Which Gospel excels in giving us the inner meaning of these events? Which of the two is more important? Is it true that the

Gospel of John stresses Christmas and Epiphany while Paul stresses Good Friday and Easter?

15. We should expect to find in the Bible at least a partial answer to which of the following questions:

a. What does it mean to be a human being?

b. What are life's ultimate issues?

c. How old is the universe?

d. Who wrote the first five books of the Bible? The Book of Isaiah?

e. Will Christ come again? When? How?

f. Will I recognize people after death?

g. Who is my neighbor?

h. Is civil disobedience ever proper?

i. Was I created by God? How?

j. Why do I need the Holy Spirit?

16. Do these assertions help us?

a. "In our own age in particular, when theology is a closed door to many people, it is a great gift to be able to preach Christ in his humanity in simple, graphic terms and to proclaim him as a member of the human race."

b. "It is sometimes destructive of faith to bombard a man with the repeated assertion that Christ is risen and leave it at that."

c. "The Church in turn exists to promote this work of Christ among men, and where it does the law disappears and the Gospel stands supreme. Christ has abolished the law of Commandments and ordinances (Ephesians 2:5) and in his risen power has himself come and preached the gospel to men (Ephesians 2:17). . . . When the Gospel is proclaimed and the Church comes into being, the dominion of the law and the relationship of wrath are ended."

d. "The weakness in Luther's approach lay in the sharp distinction which he made between 'conscience' and 'body,' or, to be more precise, in his correlation of this distinction with the fundamental distinction between gospel and law." [3]

17. Why do we have in the Bible a story like that of God testing Abraham? Didn't God know beforehand what Abraham would do? Does it tell us: Life is like this, every believer is tempted? Does it remind us: God is free to act even in ways we have never imagined or seen him act? What does it say to you?

Books for Suggested Reading

1. William D. Streng, *The Faith We Teach*. Augsburg, 1962.

2. Gustaf Wingren, *Theology in Conflict*, tr. Eric H. Wahlstrom. Muhlenberg (Fortress), 1958.

3. *The Bible: Book of Faith*. Augsburg, 1964.

4. Alvin C. Porteous, *Prophetic Voices in Contemporary Theology*. Abingdon, 1966

5. Gunther Bornkamm, *Jesus of Nazareth*. Harper, 1960.

6. H. W. Bartsch, ed., *Kerygma and Myth*, tr. Reginald H. Fuller. Harper, 1961.

CHAPTER SIX

BEARDED TRADITION

Throughout the entire period of the Old Testament no one saw clearly exactly what the future would be like. After Christ had completed his work his disciples began by looking back to discover a number of details in their past history that reminded them of Christ—all the way from the promise in Genesis 3:15 to Isaiah 53.

A similar experience puzzled many of Christ's contemporaries. After he had returned from the grave they began to understand why he had referred repeatedly to his death and resurrection.

We live in a similar period as far as the work of the Holy Spirit is concerned. He had certainly been active in the history of Israel throughout the period of the Jewish Testament; his further coming had even been foretold there.

Jesus had spoken freely and repeatedly of the work, the importance, the uniqueness, of the Spirit.

And on the Day of Pentecost he came—not as they had expected, but as God had planned. It's a power-packed story, and it reminds us once again that God's thoughts are much higher than our thoughts—that is, we can never fathom God's plans unless he reveals them to us.

We are still in the process of discovering what God attempted to do for us in the sending of his Spirit (Acts 2). Peter and the apostles met with ridicule because they did not proceed according to the tradition of the scribes and the Pharisees. By mocking, "These men are full of new wine," listeners could evade ultimate issues.

The question is not only: Why do we encounter so little ridicule? but also: If we are persecuted, is it because we have lived ultimates or because we have absolutized something peripheral: architecture, robes, our views?

There is a strange association in Scripture of Spirit and intoxication. "Be not drunk with wine but be filled with the Spirit." This is not a lesson on temperance but a reference to the fact that as alcoholics are completely under the control of "spirits," so God's people are under the influence of his Spirit. "The man of the spirit is mad" (Hosea 9:7).

At Pentecost all human distinctions vanish. "From every nation under heaven" they had come to Jerusalem. Even though this may have been an exaggeration, it did include Parthians and Medes and Elamites and others. How varied were the colors of their skins? To what extent did they differ in socio-economic backgrounds? No one thought of asking these questions; when God's Holy Spirit takes over, all human distinctions vanish. Pentecost produced a congregation, not segregation.

Now even the sexes are equal. A momentous statement, which we consider a commonplace detail, is given in Acts 1:14, "All these with one accord devoted themselves to prayer, together with the women and Mary the mother of Jesus, and with his brothers." For polemical reasons we have underscored the fact that Jesus had brothers. It may be more helpful to notice the other phrase, "together with the women." For that primitive day, when there was no woman's suffrage, this was unusual. In some churches today women are still not recognized as being equal before God. Males do not serve God in the ordained ministry because they are males but because the Holy Spirit can make them bearers of the good news. The Holy Spirit can also control the spirit of women. If the above is taken seriously, then we have to question whether any congregation which presumes to vote on whether one's color of skin is proper for membership, or one's sex for ordination, is still the church. It may be a club but it is not the church, for the church's head is Jesus Christ who rules through his Spirit.

The Book

One of the first salutary accomplishments of the Holy Spirit was the gathering of the books of the New Testament. As had occurred among the people of the Jewish Testament, the question arose repeatedly: What actually happened? What did Jesus say? What was Peter's response?

As long as the apostles who had lived with Christ were alive they could serve as resource people. But they could not be everywhere—some of them had died, and false teachers had proclaimed strange messages, so that the need for authentic documents had become quite acute. A few letters had been written by Paul and others. Then the various Gospels were recorded, stressing different aspects or purposes of Jesus' ministry.

Finally the church had to decide which books were to serve as an authentic record of what had happened and how the events were to be interpreted. Since there were many good documents available, this became an agonizing decision. Led by the Holy Spirit, the church decided about 200 A.D. the list of books to be included in the Bible (called the canon). With the completion of the New Testament the revelation of God in Christ was "closed," as it were. That's why the Bible is valued so highly among Christians. Hence we ought not be unduly disturbed if someone asks whether the canon could be enlarged in our day. This is up to the Holy Spirit. The question is purely academic, however, for it is most improbable that the whole Christian church could agree on any change. Correctly understood, it remains true, "There is no higher authority to which we can appeal beyond Scripture." [1]

Interpretation

Of equal importance is the question: How are we to interpret the Bible? It is difficult to hear the Scriptures—in fact, it is impossible without the guidance of the Spirit. But two interpreters may find something contradictory in the Scriptures and yet both claim to be controlled by God's Holy Spirit.

This may remind us how extremely reticent and careful we must be when we speak of the Holy Spirit. We do not control him; he comes to us at a time that he chooses. It is for us to be ready when he is ready.

Traditionally the church has said that the Spirit comes to us through the Word and the Sacraments. It's a simple matter to make such an assertion. It is impossible to "prove" it, and for many this statement has become an unnecessary stumbling-block, largely because of the dictatorial way in which it has often been made by people who assumed they had "a corner" on the Holy Spirit. He is probably much more prolific, creative, and unharnessed than we have assumed. As the people of the First Covenant could not see clearly the image of the promised Messiah, and as the contemporaries of Christ were puzzled by many of his promises, so we see only dimly, as through a dark glass, how the Holy Spirit is carrying God's plan forward to completion.

From the moment the canon of Scriptures had been completed and accepted, variations arose as to its interpretation. These gave rise to bitter struggles among people who were primarily to love one another! But that's the way life is, for not many listen to the Holy Spirit.

Some, for instance, said that Jesus was not really God; others said that he had not been truly human. Bitter disputes gave rise to our creeds, which were written to stress certain aspects of the faith.

All of this indicates how difficult it is to remain true to the original. The danger is that we become one-sided, for if our communication of the Gospel is spirit-filled, it will include both reverence for the traditional truth and an attempt to think it through anew for this moment.

There's no doubt about it, the Scriptures bear witness to a proclamation which occurred long ago. Those who overstress their veneration for this tradition keep on proclaiming it in a form of language which has become incomprehensible, anachronistic. This mere recitation of traditional words is an extremely deceptive kind of idolatry (bibliolatry). Since this approach is still popular, many are profoundly dissatisfied with the present-day proclamation of the Word of God; they find it totally irrelevant and even stifling for religious growth to keep on chanting about "the horns of the unicorns" and "taking captivity captive." This dissatisfaction has given rise to the profusion of Bible translations in our day, for we are faced with the difficulty of finding a middle course between antique and pop.[2]

Such an attempt at preserving tradition often gives seemingly trivial and inane precepts the dignity of eternal values. Why look for verses, for instance, to prove that people should not read bad books when no books were available in that day? And there is no use employing terms without knowing what they mean. What is worse is to quote phrases merely to confirm our own opinions.

The other extreme is the kind of experimentation which also obscures, since from a sense of emancipation it assumes that everything new is automatically good. To speak of "heaven" as the acceptance of our limitations and of "hell" as the refusal to accept our finitude is a mixture of faith and psychology that is fatal to the former.

All of this should remind us how extremely involved the problem is—the problem of taking what is of value from an ancient faith and presenting it with power and reality to modern man. The bishops of Holland describe their New Catechism as "a new effort to make the message of Jesus resound [catechism is Greek for re-echo] in the world of today . . . an expression of firm faith in this message and an effort to enunciate God's ineffable mystery in the language of our times." [3]

Danger of Extremism

Since this issue is vital, involved, and extremely contemporary, we must try to find some kind of help lest we be led astray by either extreme.

If the Spirit guides our interpretation of Scripture, he may well remind us to keep our faith personal. If Jesus was primarily concerned about man, and if the Spirit keeps returning us to Christ, he too will stress that Christ is our brother. In the church's history Christ's incarnation has often been minimized at the expense of his transcendence, and hence the importance of man has also receded into the background.

Faith can be kept personal as we search the Scriptures, for here God speaks to human beings. They are so human—Abraham and David and Peter. Yet God is faithful. Even the language of the Bible reveals this dual aspect in that we find both human and divine strains in it.

Recent Bible study has rediscovered an emphasis in Scripture which is of great help and may well have been under the guidance of the Spirit. This is the fact that we have a God who acts and speaks. An event, or an act of God, is like an iceberg. Much of the iceberg is under water, and an event of God has a hidden meaning which God interprets through words. There are so many recitals of God's great deeds in the Bible that it becomes difficult to make a choice. Some of them are more meaningful at certain periods in the church's history, depending upon whether Christians are persecuted or honored, for instance. And some events may suddenly become contemporary for us because of the vicissitudes in our own lives—marriage, death, temptation, illness. Hence we may often stress different events as individuals.

In order to recapture for our staccato lives some of the comfort of a long history we may need to recount statements and acts in the Old Testament about the coming Messiah. When we become tense and jittery over world conditions or over personal problems there is encouragement in the conviction that no dictator and no nation and no philosophy has ever toppled God from his throne. Our faith is not in history, however, but in history's God. There are acts and statements in the First Testament which because they hint at the Messiah's coming help us in recapturing a long view of history.

The judgment depicted in the Garden of Eden is symbolic of the final judgment of Christ. The life of Moses is reflected in the life of Christ (Hebrews 3:1-7, Luke 24:44, Acts 3:22 ff). Christ himself seemed to identify with the prophet Isaiah (Luke 22:37) and quoted him more often than any other Old Testament writer. The suffering of the prophets for righteous causes reminds us of the agonies of Christ, except that Christ can judge without making any mistakes (Isaiah 11:1-9). The redemption of Israel from Egypt is a picture of the redemption by Christ from evil (Colossians 1:13-14). Of course, many messianic references are hidden and were not recognized as such by the people who first experienced them.

In the New Testament, also, there is a consistent emphasis on acts and words of Christ. The Gospels, for instance, are not biographies, not fiction, not moralism (telling us what to do). They are an effort to record for posterity what happened and how this was to be interpreted. Even before the Gospels were written missionaries were proclaiming the Gospel in country and city. Sometimes they wrote letters to the congregations they had served. Each epistle was written for a *special* purpose, to *different* people, and to answer *distinct* problems. No single writer has every aspect of the Gospel, though each one presents certain facets of it. Acts is basically history, Galatians presents doctrines, James writes of ethical matters.

The red thread which runs through them all is the devotion of the writers to a person called Jesus Christ, a real person who lived and died and rose and was acknowledged by many as Messiah and Lord. John may speak of him as the preexistent word and Matthew may stress his kingdom, but all call him Lord, or Savior, or Son of God. Somehow through them all God's Spirit speaks to us.

Faith and Culture

Then what is the problem as far as interpretation is concerned? It is a twofold one: what were they trying to say in their ancient language and does this have any meaning for us? Unless this issue can be solved at least partially, the chasm between Christian faith and contemporary culture will continue to widen. What we are searching for is a livelier sensitivity to and understanding of the resources of our heritage, not as an academic exercise but in order to deal with a new and ominous destiny. Either there is formative and substantive power in the Christian faith for our lives today or we ought to build a niche for this faith in some museum. The accent may sometimes be more on the biblical and theological presuppositions of our faith, at other times more on the contemporary and social sides of our religion. Clearly there is a renewed emphasis today on the humanizing character of divine activity, an understanding of what God has planned in history to make human life human.

But how can this be accomplished by reverting to ancient imagery and phrases? There is a bondage in human language which we dare not ignore. Human thought simply cannot express God in all his majesty and love.

But we must also learn that not every word in the Scriptures is to be interpreted in its "vulgar sense." All through the cen-

turies Christians have been convinced that there is a deeper interpretation than the mere literal meaning, sometimes called pneu-
matic (*pneuma* means Spirit), spiritual, mystical, or symbolic.

Theologians today speak of myth and symbol, and this emphasis is depicted in popular literature also. There is a discovery
here which is most valuable.

The best exponents of "mythology" assert that mythology as
it is employed in the Bible stands in the way of modern man's
discovery of biblical truth. By biblical mythology is meant the
ancients' accepted image of the universe in terms of their physics,
cosmology, psychology, and sociology. That image or world view
is so thoroughly in conflict with the image functioning in our day
that the former inevitably alienates our age, which no longer
believes in demonic possession, witches, angels, slavery, or a
two-story universe.

What is the choice, then? Irrelevance—the repeating of ancient
meaningless phrases? Relativism, which states that there is nothing certain in this world?

No. Our task is to recouch the biblical message in harmony
with the image accepted by current man in order to be effective
in our day. We are not here to rewrite Scriptures but to reform
the expression. To modernize these ancient writings does not
mean to debunk them but to decode them. We must decide, but
our ultimate decision is not concerning an ancient or modern
language but concerning God.

Our task is to cull out the essential proclamation of God's sav-
ing act in Jesus Christ from the dated and largely unintelligible
language and thought forms of the ancient world so that we can
be genuinely addressed by God. This is not to remove the scandal and offense of the Gospel—in fact, only in this way can it
be confronted. It is simply to remove the wrong occasion for
stumbling in the manner in which Philip assisted the Ethiopian
eunuch.

In a day in which most of our thinking is shaped by science it
would be tragic to demand an acceptance of first-century world
views in order to be found by Christ. In fact, it would be a way
of denying the Reformation doctrine of justification by faith, for
then another kind of works would be required, the works of
sacrificing and suppressing the intellect and force us into "accept-

ing a view of the world in our faith and religion which we would deny in our everyday life."[4]

This is not so much an attempt to make the Bible relevant to modern man at all costs but simply to hear what it says. This will require more than piecing together historic events in their sequential order. It will mean to learn as John did to discover the inner meaning of events, even as a marriage is more than rings and flowers.

Much will depend on us whether we come with the right questions—whether, as Luther tried to stress, we start "not from above but from below." Our privilege is not primarily to unravel ancient tradition but to ask questions about our life, about what it means to be a human being and what the ultimate issues are for us in our day.

For Further Discussion

1. Do you recognize the portion of Scripture which is translated in a recent translation of the Gospels into Liverpool dialect: "Forgive yer enemies. Yr'll punish more dat way den if yer clocked 'em. So feed him if 'e wants scoff; give him a bevvy if he's thirsty."

2. What is the difference between the "fruits of the Spirit" and "the gifts of the Spirit"?

3. One ultraconservative recently threatened to leave the church because he was weary of being told that he was "out-of-date, stupid, prejudiced, living in a mental slum, wallowing in a spiritual ghetto, contemplating his navel, sunk in selfishness and having no concern for his fellowman." Who was off-side?

4. Is the church an instrument of mission or an object of mission? Does harmony in a church always indicate health?

5. How would you analyze the Spirit's efforts as he interprets the Scriptures to us? What important aspect was omitted in this chapter? Is Bible study hard work? Why study it at all?

6. Is there an institutional element included in the gifts of the Spirit in Ephesians 4, 1 Corinthians 12, Romans 12?

7. What statements of Christ are quoted in the second article of the Apostles' Creed?

8. What are these two experts trying to tell us?

a. "A wide reading of contemporary secular literature—especially of newspapers—is therefore recommended to any one desirous of understanding the Epistle to the Romans." [5]

b. "We have in Deuteronomy the most comprehensive example of a theological restatement of old traditions which in the later Israel could become at the same time the message of Yahweh." [6]

9. Does the Exodus say anything to you?

10. Is it possible to approach the Bible without presuppositions?

11. The sun rises and sets. This is a lovely expression. Is it true today? God is our Father—but he is not our Father physically— that is, literally. Then what portions of the Bible do we accept literally? Can you take the Bible's contents seriously without taking all of it literally? What is the difference between myth and fairy tale? If much of the Bible is symbolic, where do you draw the line? Are we to interpret Psalm 23 literally?

12. In interpreting the Bible, is there always a danger that we substitute a different message?

13. Did Eve eat of an apple or is Genesis 3 a symbolic affirmation of man's estrangement from God through the fact of sin? Is man estranged by creation or by sin? Are we still eating of this apple?

14. What can we learn from the Pentecostal churches as far as the revivifying and creative power of the Spirit is concerned?

15. Is this stated well: There is really no need to search out every detail of the historical Jesus. He lives today wherever man is reunited with man, wherever there is healing. Through the Spirit he now becomes my ultimate concern, as was the case with Paul.

16. Protestants believe that "the Bible is its own interpreter." Is this the same as saying, "The meaning of the Christian message which the biblical writers proclaim must not be interpreted by reference to norms that are foreign to the Bible." Give illustrations.

17. If the Bible is full of parables and symbolism, does the following become meaningful? "The road beyond psychology leads to a point where art and religion meet, join, and transform each other."[7] "Art is a lie that makes us realize the truth" (Picasso). Denis de Rougemont calls art a "trap for meditation." For further information consult: Roger Hazelton, Abingdon Press, Nashville, 1967.

18. Sometimes a figurative statement of Christ is interpreted literally, and vice versa. John, for instance, loves myth. How are the following to be interpreted: John 2:19-20; 3:3-4; 4:10-11; 6:51-52; 7:33-35; 11:11-12; 12:32-34; 13:8-9; 14:3-5; 21:22-23? What references to the Lord's Supper are to be taken figuratively? Why? In Genesis 1-11 and Romans 5 what is literary dress and what is basic message?

19. Dietrich Bonhoeffer: "It is not for us to prophesy the day (though the day will come) when men will once more be called so to utter the word of God that the world will be changed and renewed by it. It will be a new language, perhaps quite non-religious, but liberating and redeeming—as was Jesus' language; it will shock people and yet overcome them by its power; it will be the language of a new righteousness and truth, proclaiming God's peace with men and the coming of his kingdom."[8] Has this day arrived? Which is worse: to deny an article of faith or to deny help to the needy?

20. Would symbolism be a better word than myth? Smoke is a symbol of fire. A green light is a symbol.

21. The Bible bears witness to a proclamation which has happened and is the impulse for proclamation to our generation. Must this be communicated in a form of language which has become incomprehensible? Who is at fault if some of these pages are largely incomprehensible? Does Ian Ramsey's statement apply to us: "What can be said, can be said plainly. If it cannot be said plainly, we should be suspicious of its claim to be said at all."[9] How would you retell one of the parables?

22. Does Christ speak to us in contemporary events in the same way as he speaks through events in the Bible?

23. Is our conscience a clear and certain interpreter of the will

of God or of the ethical choices incumbent upon us in obedience to the will of God?

24. Did the church grow in its regard for and interpretation of the Scriptures? Had the authority of the Scriptures been self-evident, would not the canon have been self-evident?

25. Did the rich young ruler reject the implications of the Gospel because he was not willing to pay the price of commitment or because he did not understand the issues clearly?

26. If the following is true, then it should be helpful: "In Biblical history the *mythos* is not and cannot be differentiated from the actual history, and the *history* in its turn is not to be separated from the *mythos*. History becomes mythical because it is experienced in the spirit of pious imagination, instead of being the product of objective inquiry and scientific research. Biblical history is *mythological* because it narrates what God has done. At the same time, Biblical *mythos* is *historical* because it narrates what the people of God have done. Biblical history is mythological because it is the history of God's revelation addressed to His people. Revelation and religious imagination, therefore, complement each other." [10]

27. Is it true that "we live between the time of the theology which no longer makes sense to us and the time of a theology which has not yet clearly dawned"?

28. "The more a man speaks in modern terms the more he will be heard. And the more he is heard the greater will be the acceptance *and* the rejection of his message, the more provocative will it be, and the more emphatic will be the decisions and separations that result. When the Word becomes flesh then. . . ." [11]

29. What does the story of Jesus' cursing of the fig tree say to us (Mark 11:12-25)? Bertrand Russell used it to illustrate why he could not accept Jesus as the Son of God, for how could the perfect Son of God in a moment of frustration curse an innocent fig tree which he had created? Is the fig tree a symbol of the institutional aspect of Israel (Isaiah 34:1-4)? If there are no leaves, figs will not appear either. Should the church work for social changes which bear promise for the future?

Books for Suggested Reading

1. Carl F. Burke, *God Is for Real, Man.* Association, 1966.

2. William Neill, *The Rediscovery of the Bible.* Harper, 1954.

3. George W. Forell, *The Protestant Faith.* Prentice-Hall, 1960.

4. James D. Smart, *The Interpretation of the Scriptures.* Westminster, 1961.

5. Carl Michalson, *Worldly Theology: The Hermeneutical Focus of an Historical Faith.* Scribner, 1967.

CHAPTER SEVEN

HAS THE CHURCH
BETRAYED CHRIST?

Jesus spoke much of God's kingdom.
But what do we have today?
The church.
Say this with a sneer and you are echoing an extremely popular
contemporary conviction. Is there any connection left between the
loving, serving, lowly Christ and a proud, wealthy, elite institution called the church? Has not the church—divided, weak, un-
loving, isolated—betrayed the one whom she was to serve and
proclaim?

This is a deadly charge that cannot be ignored. Neither should
it be pushed aside in cavalier fashion as if it were asked only
by those who are against God. Some devoted church people are
passionately concerned with this same issue. We cannot offer the
final and all-inclusive answer here, but a few thoughts and guidelines might be of value to those of us who are concerned about
ultimate issues for ourselves and our children. We should always
be conscious of the fact that pure protest unleavened by constructive proposals is for the birds.

Has the church been faithful to her Lord?

We could evade the issue by engaging in a profound discussion
as to what it means to be "faithful," who the church is, and
whether anyone knows who the real Christ was. Why dance
around the issue?

A Theology of Change

Intelligent people do not expect the church of today, with almost half a billion members, to be an exact replica of Christ's small group of disciples. We cannot all get into the Upper Room, nor do we live in a primitive culture or speak Aramaic. If the God-man Christ were living today, he would be doing different works and speaking a different language. Where there is life and growth there is bound to be change. To return to this early way of life as shepherds and cobblers, without sanitation and electricity, is neither possible nor desirable.

But neither can we envision a church which has little or nothing to do with the Christ of the first century. If the organized church has betrayed him, then she no longer has the right to call herself church or Christian. There is enough truth in the critical statements about the church to make us wince and examine.

Christ was loving and energetic. He spoke of a kingdom which was not of this world, and yet healed people for this world. He could do miracles but did them very sparingly. The church, on the other hand, is concerned about buildings and budgets instead of people. Such statements ought to be examined carefully as to the degree of their validity.

How did the church begin? Not even the experts agree. In a way it began with Christ's incarnation, or on the night of his betrayal when he instituted the Lord's Supper, or on Easter, or on Pentecost (which is usually celebrated as the birthday of the Christian church).

The Christian church and the Holy Spirit are closely allied, for it is the Spirit who came in fullest measure on the Day of Pentecost. As he somehow in a mysterious manner guided people to gather the documents of the Bible, so he led men and women and children into a community of love, a fellowship of the Spirit, a communion of saints, which more and more came to be known as the church. Need we pause to underscore here that the church is not a building or even primarily an organization but a group of people who confess that Christ is their Lord?

Has the church possibly fulfilled her purpose in history? Is it time that other groups take over from here?

Could be. And maybe not.

To gloat about the church's glorious history—and in many ways it served mankind—is not of much help at this moment.

Are there any dynamic ultimates which can be found in and through the church? That depends upon whether the church is true to her original purpose.

Where Christ is, there is the church. Many definitions have been given of the church, but this seems to be valid: Christ and his church ought not to be separated. The church has a divine purpose, and the degree to which she serves God she is the church. The Holy Spirit is eager and ready to build a community of love among us as vital and authentic and relevant as any in the past. Every reformation rests on the work of the Holy Spirit, and it may well be that the next great reformation will come when we shall be ready to receive in fuller measure what the Spirit has to offer.

But the church is for imperfect people, and hence she can and does make miserable mistakes. This was true already in the first century, when the apostles had to remind Christians not to give special honor to the wealthy in the Sunday service and that incest is not to be condoned in the fellowship of Christ. You will recall other instances of this kind.

And through the centuries this has become even more of a temptation and a real possibility. One of the most critical periods in the history of the Christian church came after the end of the persecutions. Suddenly—in 311—under Constantine a maligned, despised, dispossessed group was lifted to a place of honor, for as soon as the emperor had been converted church membership became a mark of distinction. The Gospel spread feverishly, often because membership in the church was socially desirable or even forced. Now wars were fought for Christ, and the Emperor intervened in church affairs. Monasteries arose in an attempt by Christians to get away from secular authority, but these touched the lives of only a small minority.

The year 1054 was another fatal one; then the church was divided into Eastern and Western. There were bright days in the history of the church, both East and West, and many dark ones.

Then, in the sixteenth century, came the Protestant Reformation of Martin Luther, John Calvin, and others. It was a turbulent period, for intense personalities fought for their ultimate concerns. Christians gathered into groups according to their convictions—Roman Catholics, who were determined to remain loyal to their church; the followers of Luther, who emphasized the Bible's proclamation of justification by faith; adherents of John Calvin, with a consistent and strong declaration of the sovereignty and majesty of God; Enthusiasts, who emphasized the work and power of the Holy Spirit in the lives of individuals; and many smaller groups which arose in subsequent centuries.

Again this portion of the history of the church presents heroes of the first order and squabbles and petty arguments which in no way honor the cause of Christ. The devotion and suffering, for instance, of countless missionaries who attempted to bring the love of Christ to other cultures are beyond our power of description.

But probably never in her history has the church been under such attack from within and without as in our day. The reasons are many, but somehow they culminate in the charge that the Christian church has betrayed Jesus Christ.

Every one of us will have to come to our own convictions in this matter. It may well be that—as so often in her history—the church, both corporately and as individuals, has denied her Lord by not listening to the pleas of the Holy Spirit. And it may also well be that—as so often in the past—there is a remnant, there are prophets, there is a Word, there is a Holy Spirit, all of whom can show the way toward reform and renewal to those who have ears to hear.

For Further Discussion

1. Was the church important in the thinking of Christ?

2. Is it true that the church
      ——is infallible?
      ——is to serve people?
      ——has a tradition to preserve?
      ——is true to the Bible?
      ——is overorganized?
      ——ought to pay tax on property?
      ——has betrayed Christ?

3. Is Colin Williams correct in his assertion: "We therefore have this ironic but tragic fact, that in many instances the resi-

dence parish congregation is popular precisely because it is irrelevant!"? [1]

4. Does this express our feelings? "It is often a mark of the Protestant who has seen some of the meaning of 'religionless Christianity' that he has constantly to make up his mind on Sunday morning whether the irritation which he will experience if he goes to church is less intolerable than the sense of frustration and guilt he will have if he stays at home." [2]

5. Is Eugene Carson Blake right when he states, "Why didn't the church stay that way, just informal gatherings under informal leadership of God-directed men and women?" Because of murmuring (Acts 6) "they had to begin the organization of the church." Also: "Many fearful conservatives do not realize that the restatement of the ancient biblical faith and its defense is in fact the number one duty of the church in our time." [3]

6. To worship "in Spirit and in truth" should help us overcome the bane of ritual cosmetics since the Spirit insures

a. that Christ is not a mere memory but a living reality who confronts me at every moment of my life,

b. that worship is not a matter of manipulation but responding to One who always takes the initiative, and

c. that worship is primarily corporate, never apart from the Spirit's fellowship. What important aspect should be added?

7. If we attack the church and some of its progressive leaders, could we be attacking the wrong enemy? Is the local parish like a branch office, or is it headquarters?

8. On the Mount of Transfiguration Peter suggested that the apostles build three tabernacles so that they could dwell there in the shining light of their Lord. Jesus did not dwell in peaceful isolation. How does organization help or hinder in this purpose?

9. Who will present a brief history of Constantine's influence on the church?

10. What caused the great division in 1054? How were the Eastern and Roman Catholic churches partially reconciled in our day?

11. Who are the Enthusiasts? Have they any successors today? What is their great contribution in our age to the universal Christian church?

12. "A church which avoids politics, or worse still, uses politics will never speak to secular man" (Dietrich Bonhoeffer).

13. "We have too many managers and too few freedom fighters" (Dr. Ernest Kaesemann). Is this charge true of the church, my denomination, my parish?

14. Do we feel more threatened when we discuss Communism or hunger, Buddhism or disease? Why?

15. The great Bernard of Clairvaux wrote to his friend the Pope, "You let yourself be overwhelmed by judgments that you must pass in all kinds of external and worldly matters. I hear of nothing but judgments and 'laws' from you. All that, and striving after esteem and wealth, comes from Constantine, not from Peter." What would you write to your superiors?

16. Can the church be compared to the Prodigal Son?

17. What can we do if we find the actions of our church body or some utterances of our pastor unpalatable? What does love require? Which of my most cherished beliefs have I surrendered because they were subjected to searching criticism?

18. What are "open questions"? List a few.

19. In 1853 *The Independent,* a Protestant Journal, was advocating a program of urban renewal and the Federal Council of Churches was promoting the church's entrance into social problems. At the time the editors were chastised severely. Has the church erred more often on the side of conservatism or change?

20. Does Ezra 3:10-13 apply to our situation? Jeremiah 7:4?

21. When a slum landlord, a racist, or a profiteer joins the church what should happen? Could you ever vote to excommunicate someone?

22. "Many Lutheran and Reformed Christians are not at all clear why Lutherans and Reformed Churches cannot form a

unity, since the confessional differences are no longer a live issue in their consciousness. Only theologians with historical and theological knowledge are in a position to formulate the differences precisely and to conduct conversations about their confessions." [4] Is there anything unique about your denomination?

23. What is your reaction to this statement: "The poverty question comes up in many ways: Should the church remain largely as one of the 'helping agencies' and thereby continue its traditional social-service view of poverty? Should it cast its lot with non-governmental organizers, such as Saul Alinsky, investing money, staff, and prestige in building political power for the poor? These, not the Virgin Birth or the inerrancy of Scripture, are the issues church leaders discuss most ferociously today." [5]

24. "It is evident that when the churches are most deeply involved in standing on the side of the poor and oppressed, and in serving human needs of every kind, they are forced to think, act and live together." [6]

25. "There is no doubt that the social gospel has directed its energies toward the release of many of the problems of suffering humanity. I am for it! I believe it is biblical." [7]

26. Money and sex and delinquents and homos and ghettos and suburbia—are these all included in the church's agenda? In what area are we strong or weak?

27. F. W. Dillistone emphasizes that if each individual functions properly in relation to the whole and the whole functions properly insofar as each individual is related to it then the church is the church. In your background have these two been properly balanced? Is there a "real presence" of Jesus apart from his people? Did Jesus stress the individual or the group in the parable of the lost coin, the lost sheep, the prodigal son? If the individual is disproportionately exalted, we get a revivalistic pietism; if he is disproportionately degraded, we end up with political totalitarianism. Does the Spirit dwell in individuals or in the fellowship? Nothing is more individual than the body (can I love someone I cannot touch?), and nothing is more organic and social. Where does Paul stress this?

28. Did not the Reformation place a strong emphasis on the individual's uninhibited access to God? Then how do you explain the following: "The Holy Christian Church is the principal work of God for the sake of which all things were made,"[9] and "I take God and his angels to witness, never since I became a teacher of the church have I had any other purpose than the church's advancement."[10]

29. Why do people outside the organized church seem to get along as well as those within it?

30. How has your faith changed in the last ten years?

31. Is this a valid response in church: "I like things the way they are"?

32. Is this a dilemma and how are we involved in it? "Man is created for fellowship with God, a fellowship which is broken by sin and which can be restored in a relationship of faith in Christ. How one *communicates* this to the world of the twentieth century is the issue."[11]

33. How do you respond to statements such as the following which we cannot avoid hearing in our day:

a. "The main task of evangelism is to keep people out of the church building."[12]

b. "What is the use of getting more people into a church that is no church?"[13]

c. "The Church is saying to itself—prophecy without involvement is for the birds."[14]

d. "Every testimony to Christ without reference to the world will lack reality, every statement about the world unrelated to Christ will fall short of the truth."[15]

e. A Negro youth in Harlem asked the speaker during a meeting on non-violence, "What's all this Jesus crap?"[16]

f. "The starting point for any theology of the church today must be a theology of social change."[17]

g. The work of God in the world, where Jesus Christ is present, is like a "floating crap game," and the church is like a confirmed gambler whose "major compulsion upon arising each day is to know where the action is" so he can run there and "dig it."[18]

h. Paul in 1 Corinthians 13.

i. "It is the minister of the local church who lives and works in the most exposed, dangerous place among all the so-called religious 'professionals,' because he is literally on the firing line, and he must bear the brunt of the opposition toward, and the denial of, the gospel in face-to-face confrontation." [19]

j. "Psychotherapy can put a person back on the right track . . . but religion can show him that the track goes somewhere. When a religious person is suffering deep emotional consequences of real guilt, a good psychiatrist will send him to his clergyman. Chances are, he is seeking forgiveness and not psychoanalysis. Conversely, if the distress is brought on by imagined guilt that has no basis in reality, a good clergyman will send him to a psychiatrist." [20]

k. " . . . The deadness of the church in these times, yes, deadness despite its seeming prosperity, is because even the men inside it do not comprehend the revolutionary implications of that affirmation. They may go on saying creeds and singing hymns, and trying to work out some little niche for religion in their personal lives. But it is all so much nostalgic hogwash if the excitement and unbelievable implication of the confession of Christ as Lord and Savior do not take hold of a man's mind and heart. . . .

It ought to make a difference, a visible difference, if a man says he belongs to that peculiar tribe of people who have chosen to pin their life to Jesus Christ. It ought not to be, by the same token, a kind of uniform that identifies a man as a member of a special organization who chooses to exercise certain esoteric tastes, or arrogates to himself superior virtue because he bears the stamp of celestial approval. This is always the temptation— to turn faithful obedience into an inflexible armor to shut out the assaults of uncertainty and insecurity that life in this world brings as surely as the dawn—for the Christian as well as the non-Christian.

To be a Christian in any age, and this one is no exception, is to be fully a man—a creature of God, not isolated and sterilized by your religion, but responding as a whole being to the times and the people among whom one is set. It means further responding as one who has been freed by Jesus Christ to take a chance, to be experimental, to laugh at fate and cry with compassion, to work and to play: in short, to be a new creature, born of a new birth." [21]

l. The church is most true to itself when it is least concerned about its own welfare. By maintaining its own purity and integrity as the household of God, the church is doing a good thing; but by going out from itself, bearing the food and drink of the Gospel, the church is doing a better thing. Which of these two has priority? Which needs special emphasis in our day?

m. Nothing is more important than our fellow man.

n. What we see is largely determined by where we stand.

34. Does this help? Secularization is a process or a liberating development in which we are freed from a closed religious or metaphysical world-view. It finds its roots in the biblical faith and is open to change and to involvement. Secularism is a closed system which keeps us in bondage to this world.

35. "Evangelism is witness. It is one beggar telling another beggar where to get food. The Christian does not offer out of his bounty. He has no bounty. He is simply a guest at his Master's table and, as evangelist, he calls others too. The evangelistic relation is to be 'alongside of,' not 'over against.' The Christian stands alongside the non-Christian and points to the gospel, the holy action of God. It is not his knowledge of God that he shares, it is to God himself that he points." [22]

36. What is the role of world missionaries in our day? Which of these two statements of churchmen comes closest to your convictions? Why?

a. "The era of the foreign missionary movement is definitely over because the goals and objectives of that movement are no longer valid" (Rev. Ronan Hoffman).

b. "While the Church must indeed serve the world, it can best do so by performing its own distinctive kind of service, namely to bring men the fruits of Christ's redemptive action through word and sacrament, teaching and example" (Rev. Avery Dulles).

37. Since Christ is everywhere, we do not bring him to distant peoples but we expose them to the reality of Christ in their midst. If this is true, how does it change our efforts in mission?

Books for Suggested Reading

1. Stephen Rose, *Who's Killing the Church?* Association, 1966.

2. Martin E. Marty, *Second Chance for American Protestants.* Harper, 1963.

3. Gibson Winter, *The New Creation as Metropolis.* Macmillan, 1963.

4. Roland Bainton, *The Reformation of the Sixteenth Century.* Beacon, 1956.

5. Sir George MacLeod, *Only One Way Left.* Iona Community, Glasgow, Iowa, 1956.

6. Eugene Carson Blake, *The Church in the Next Decade.* Macmillan, 1966.

7. Paul Minear, *Images of the Church in the New Testament.* Westminster, 1960.

8. Pierre Payne, *The Holy Fire.* Harper, 1957.

9. Rex R. Dolan, *The Big Change.* Westminster, 1968.

10. Saul Alinsky, *The Ways of a Professional Agitator.*

CHAPTER EIGHT

DIALOGUE WITHOUT PREJUDICE

Why is there so much disturbance in the church? This ought not alarm us unduly, for where there is life there is action; where the Spirit of God is at work, there is disquiet. Even disputes may be a sign that the church lives and proof that controversy can enrich. In fact, one of the distinguishing and encouraging marks of our generation has been a readiness to subject established institutions and values to critical reevaluation. Those who are reasonably certain about the basics of their faith need not be overly concerned about peripheral changes. Between apathy and panic we may serve men best by asking: How should we decide? Shall we ignore the church, reform it under God, or maintain the status quo?

A few of the major thrusts at renewal are beginning to crystallize. These are, of course, based on the firm conviction that the church is worth renewing, that it has a message for our day, that it does help solve basic concerns of human existence. Possibly, like Christ, the church will have to sacrifice itself in order to serve.

While no attempt is made to arrange these suggested changes in order of importance, and while new emphases are emerging constantly, it may be possible to cull out those which are of real value today in our situation.

Servanthood and Pietism

One of the wholesome tensions which is struggling for clarification and implication in our concern for a vital church is the dialectic between servanthood and pietism. Unless one has come to some degree of understanding in this matter many of the other issues will remain clouded. It is extremely difficult to dialogue in this matter without prejudice and yet with passion.

On one of his journeys Jesus met a charming individual— wealthy, refined, cultured, well-behaved. In the ensuing dialogue (Mark 10:17-22) Jesus accepted the young man's assertion that he had kept all the commandments from his youth. And yet Christ, whose ministry was based on love, sensed a deep lack in his life, for the man was not quite ready to follow him.

This parable may be applied to the church. The church is afflu- ent—it has built colleges and missions—yet is there something lacking? Of course there is, for perfection is never reached on this side of the stars. But Christ still loves his church and is eager to have his people follow him.

Such following, however, involves suffering and servanthood. Pietism, on the other hand, loves to confine its faith to private spheres, shying away from the centers of life.

The difference has also been described as that of a redeeming or a redeemed community.

Theologically and historically the usual definition of the church has been "where the Word is preached and the Sacraments are rightly administered." This is a valid and vital definition of the church "gathered." But there is another dimension of the church which must be added lest we have a truncated view, and that is the dimension of mission. A "come" church must at the same time be a "go" church.

Pietism prefers to stress individual acts, servanthood service to men. While the church exists wherever the Word is preached and the Sacraments are administered, it is also a people in whom Christ is being formed. And while servants may and should spe- cialize, there is no preeminence in the sight of God.

No Structure Has Validity

Structure is important and necessary, but no structure has per- manent validity. On the functional level this kind of statement is extremely difficult to implement.

It is impossible for people to function without organization. This is equally applicable to the church. God planned the salva-

tion of man; Christ chose an order of procedure which prompted
him to go up to Jerusalem at a certain time; he asked Peter and
John to go ahead and prepare a room, dusting tables and arrang-
ing cups, so that he could institute the Lord's Supper. All these
required organization.

But form follows function. The church must be quite free and
flexible in seeking new forms.

Here we have much to learn from the prophets for whom form
is not only secondary but very often demonic when it tries to
usurp the place of ultimates. Amos and Jeremiah, Isaiah and
Ezekiel, seem to say that the spirit, the heart, our motivation, our
faith, is much more important than structure. In his cavalier manner Luther could strike out at church superiors and time-honored
structures which he felt were no longer honoring Christ, and he
did it in a way which his followers ought to recapture.

One of the aspects of this attempt to find the proper niche for
organization is the agony over the disquieting question: Is the
parish structure still valid for our day? Many salvos have been
fired in this battle, and sociologists have helped to sharpen the
tools. These skillful thrusts, administered with loving concern
and often with brutal honesty, expose real weaknesses and explore
basic motifs.

For the first thousand years of her history the church had no
territorial parishes as we know them. These developed because
of the social cohesiveness of villages and clusters of population in
the Middle Ages. Reactions to the typical parish structure fall
roughly into the following:

a. There are those who vigorously defend the present shape of
the parish. What we need is simply more of same. Some seem to
defend present congregational polity as a kind of divinely ordained sacred cow which must not be questioned or changed, as
though the Gospel would suffer if the form were changed.

b. Another group has apparently given up on the traditional
form of the parish as being simply unable to sustain Christ's ministry of reconciliation in the modern era. These critics heavily
underscore industrial chaplaincies, lay retreats, health and welfare agencies, urban planning, high-rise or even underground
ministries. Experts in this group have sociological analyses to
support their contention. Not all in this group are simply angry

young men; many are serving with an uncalculating generosity and constructive self-giving that demands respect and admiration. Hence the question is not really: How do we renew our congregation but: What is our mission at this place in our day? This may mean supporting and encouraging new forms in order to be present at points of decision and need, whether this be the power structures of our day or teen-age groups searching for meaning and identity.

c. More toward the center are those who do not appear to question the basic structure of the parish. Though the parish in their view may become obsolete and relatively unimportant in the future shape of the church's purpose, it may also continue to serve in more settled areas. Not structural obsolescence but inner conversion and commitment are the basic problems. More than the structure of the church is under judgment. If the church regains a sense of mission and servanthood, structures will emerge to serve that purpose.

A self-study in this area is in order. Love for Christ and for people does not require a cynical rejection of the parish structure, at least not until a better alternative has been proposed. Nor ought we take a defensive stance which is against change in peripheral matters. Change is in order when it is linked with a sense of responsible stability.

In fact, much of the discussion about structure, establishment, and organization may be an evidence of the poverty of our theology. It would be difficult to picture normal parents spending most of their time telling friends how many pairs of shoes they have purchased for their children through the years and how many hamburgers. The children, their growth and welfare, are our concern, and not the organizational details. A people which is engaged in ultimate concerns will find the best structures for their particular tasks in their particular situation. At times it is necessary to take one's own temperature or to repair one's car, but these are never ends in themselves. Even church renewal is not our primary concern; rather it is human renewal. Whichever structure serves the latter should be adopted. The Holy Spirit can supply ingenuity and flexibility, but these are, however, only prerequisites for servanthood and involvement.

Ecumenics

More than organizational structure is involved in another thrust related to the church, usually referred to as the Ecumenical Movement. It is supported by many on the basis of doctrinal grounds. Did not Christ pray (John 17), "Holy Father, keep them in thy name which thou hast given me, that they may be one, even as we are one"? Others support this movement on the basis of the needs of men—unless the church unites in its efforts for mankind it may fail even more than it has. A church which is divided can hardly tell others to love one another. And the more a church believes that it has the truth the more it ought to share what it has with others. Many are reticent to join in ecumenical ventures because of the conviction that this leads to syncretism. The choice we cannot escape.

Among the first to promote unity among the churches was the Ecumenical Patriarch of Constantinople, who in 1920 issued an encyclical calling upon all the churches "To meet together, regardless of their confessional differences, in one Koinonia of churches, in order that they might, through this Koinonia, face the problems with which the modern world confronts them." Out of this initiative, together with other voices and movements, the World Council of Churches was constructed. Soon contacts were also made with Roman Catholicism. Intensive dialog has continued to our day, increasing constantly in depth and intensity.

As with any great effort so also with ecumenism—when it comes down to earth in practical situations it becomes most difficult. To practice ecumenism on the local level requires much patience, ingenuity, and Christian concern.

The final answer has not been given in this matter, but two major thrusts seem to be emerging, especially as far as the inner city is concerned. In rural areas many small parishes of various denominations have merged as the only alternative, and some have found it an exhilarating experience.

In heavily populated areas these attempts seem to contain promise.

a. Use present structures.

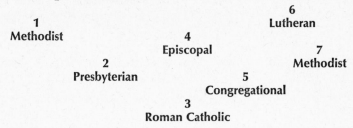

6
Lutheran

1
Methodist

4
Episcopal

7
Methodist

2
Presbyterian

5
Congregational

3
Roman Catholic

In this effort No. 1 may become a center to serve the aged; No. 2 for Youth Activities and Education for Adults; No. 3 Education for Elementary Grades and Junior High; No. 4, since it is the largest, may serve as worship center with many and varied worship services throughout the week; No. 5 as a Counseling Center with accredited psychiatrists on call, and a family oriented congregation; No. 6 could serve as liaison with community agencies; and No. 7 for experimental ministries.

b. Another plan envisions cooperation in one cluster of buildings.

megalopolis

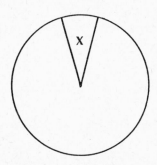

In this plan the local parish is definitely the center of religious concern. In fact, everyone in that sector becomes the concern of the parish. At this center worship services are conducted, cooperatively, probably by denominations for the time being. Full-time counselors, pastors, psychiatrists, and educators serve throughout the week. Professionals in the suburbs, such as lawyers and medics, are available in Christian service to the poverty-stricken in the inner city. Cells can be developed in outlying areas for

Bible study and community action. On special festivals the entire parish may worship together in one grand service of intercession and praise.

It may be that our first responsibility consists of listening to one another. Knowledge may refer to truth and proposition, but listening is always personal. The ecumenical aspect of religious education has often consisted primarily of supplying fair and sympathetic information about other religious bodies. Now this must be followed by an actual joining of hands in the service of human needs and of reconciliation in a divided world. All our teaching should be informed by a sense of history and of change so that we present our respective traditions as always developing and never as a perfect expression of the Christian faith. Then loyalty and love for a particular denomination can serve and be combined with genuine openness and ecumenical passion. The roots of such an effort will reach the ultimates of our faith.

Beyond the Walls

In some ways many Christians have attempted to engage in dialogue with those of other faiths. At first some felt this to be a burdensome responsibility, only to discover that it can also be a summons to responsible maturity and of real service to mankind. The most fundamental notion about a dialogue as a model of educational action is that it is an action between friends and not mere disputants.

There is much also that we have in common with the Jews, from Jesus and Paul to Martin Buber and Marc Chagall.

When does tolerance become disloyalty? Every man must answer this in his own way. But certainly strife and hatred are not God-pleasing either. Hence there is an attempt also to understand religions such as Islam, with its consistent concern about transgression of natural law; Buddhism, which makes a devoted effort to correct misconduct by one's own efforts; humanism, with its conviction that offenses against man are inhuman. Vatican II underscored this effort with the assertion: "The Church rejects, as foreign to the mind of Christ, any discrimination against men or harassment of them because of their race, colour, condition of life or religion."

Occasionally there are also attempts to dialogue with Marxists rather than to increase tension and struggle between them. While we have chafed under the assertion of Karl Marx that "Religion is the opium of the people," we dare not ignore the fact that he had just read in St. Augustine's *City of God* the statement: "God introduced slavery in the world as a punishment of sin. Therefore it would be against his will to suppress it." Either we can race toward mutual self-destruction or we can learn to live together and possibly learn from one another. Both Christians and Marxists claim to be intensely concerned about man's future and welfare, about human personality in its integrity. Both have, of course, on occasion failed to offer what they claim to offer. But this dialogue may determine the destiny and nature of our children and grandchildren. Even if there were no nuclear threat, Christians and Marxists should be conversing, not only to avoid nuclear destruction but to affirm life and make it livable for more people.

"If Catholics [Christians] try to deepen their faith . . . and if Marxists try to absorb into their vision of the world the dimension of subjectivity, of transcendence, which Christianity has brought into it, there are, I think, possibilities of convergence. In other words, if a Catholic is a better Catholic, and a Marxist a better Marxist, the dialogue will be made easier." Karl Marx: "The philosophers have only *interpreted* the world . . . the point, however, is to *change* it." [1] What happens to our efforts at conversion when the same author asserts: "It is an incontestable fact of our age that the future of man cannot be constructed either against religious believers or without them. Neither can it be constructed against the Communists or without them." What is the difference between conversion, confrontation, convergence?

For Further Discussion

1. What's good about the church? About the world?
2. Can the church be compared to an Indian Reservation? To a ghetto?
3. What is meant by "kenosis"? This Greek word summarizes the thrust of Philippians 2:7.
4. Why have students in our universities been enrolling in

record numbers in courses of religion? Which do we sometimes prefer: prescriptions or pain killers?

5. What organizational structures in your parish are serving the servanthood of members? Are assertions such as this true—a church meeting which does not help people is a sheer waste and self-deception?

6. Simply going to church does not make one a Christian, Luther remarked and added, "Dogs also occasionally stray into church and remain dogs as before."

7. What is the difference between piety and pietism? What does the expression "holy worldliness" say to you?

8. As far as time permits what do these men have to offer in the area of parish renewal:

Peter Berger	Martin Marty	Martin Buber
Gibson Winter	William Stringfellow	Robert Raines
G. W. Webber	Elton Trueblood	John Mott

9. Why does Paul write to the Thessalonians: "Our gospel came to you not in word only"?

10. What is the difference between debate and dialog? Is dialogue more than good will? "Dialogue is an objective necessity of the age." [2] Why did Luther stress the "mutual conversation and consolation of the brethren? Who helped him? Can there be any dialogue if you insist that your understanding is the correct one? Is there a more threadbare and stale discussion than when someone's convictions are exclusive?

11. "Whenever the church loses its capacity for dialogue with contemporary thought and culture, it becomes opinionated in its views of the world, dogmatic in its understanding and statement of faith, and irrelevant in its teaching." [3]

12. How does your parish function in the public sector? What can we learn from the Detroit Industrial Mission, East Harlem Protestant Parish, Los Angeles Regional Goals Project, Metropolitan Association of Philadelphia?

13. How do you react to the following statements as far as they refer to ecumenical endeavors:

a. Our starting point is always Trinitarian and Christocentric.

b. Our unity must become manifest, tangible, so that it is more than a lovely feeling.

c. Only if there is renewal in all churches can there be unity.

d. Unity must enable us to perform better our mission to the world, also in social and international affairs.

e. This must be a movement of churches rather than individuals.

f. Men refuse to take orders today, hence this cannot become a superchurch.

g. Religious liberty has come to stay.

h. Our problems are people, not fat books of theology.

i. The keyword is not unity but koinonia (1 Corinthians 12).

j. Theologians are more responsible than lay people for holding back.

k. There is more variety within churches than among churches.

l. If reconciliation and authentic community constitute God's gift to the world, then a dismembered church contravenes its own message.

m. The task and challenge of serving the inner city and vast rural areas is too massive and too complex for any group to tackle alone.

n. There is no dialogue which does not change the participants.

13. "The day may come when Christians will gather in accord with their common tasks and localities rather than in accord with their shades of doctrine." [4] "When men and women join together in mission, divisions and denominational differences no longer make sense, and joining in the task becomes a celebration of unity—a working together in joy in the service of Christ and our brothers." [5]

14. If there is a conflict between what the organized church suggests and your service to fellow human beings, the evangelical response would be in favor of the latter. Give an illustration of this, preferably from your own experience.

15. "No contemporary movement in Protestantism is so strong as that of the aspiration to church unity." [6] Is this true in your area?

16. In *Unitive Protestantism*, John T. McNeill maintains that the ecumenical concern for unity is "primarily to be explained as the outcropping of an element original to Protestantism, though hitherto largely frustrated." [7] What does this say to us?

17. Are these assertions still true?

a. "The purest churches under heaven are subject both to mixture and to error. . . . Nevertheless, there shall be always a Church on earth to worship God according to his will." [8]

b. "It is the will of God that the communion of his Church should be maintained in the external society." [9]

c. The koinonia of God's people is not identical with the empirical church nor separable from it. One ought to correct and strengthen and cleanse the other.

d. The priesthood of believers is not individualistic but communal through and through.

e. Life with God is intensely personal but never isolated, for it always brings fellowship with it.

f. He who is reasonably certain of basics does not have to be overly concerned about structures.

18. After suggesting that what happens to the Jews is a symbol of what usually happens to mankind a generation later, a Jewish theologian maintained that the rabbi will become more a teacher and less an administrator in his congregation. The synogogue is to become more a center for learning than a place for clubs and even less a place for prayer, since, "I think we may be nagging God too much with prayer." [10]

19. How should the Christian church relate to the Jews or to the other three major religions: Hinduism, Buddhism, Islam? How does the following differ from former attitudes? After discussing great cultures of the past the authors state, "And we may be sure that our Lord Jesus Christ, the eternal Word, was at work in the wisdom of these religions, through his Holy Spirit: not manifestly, as God revealed him coming among the Jews, but no doubt really and profoundly." [11]

20. "No repetition of the positions in the debates about the apostolic ministry during the past hundred years will be equal to the situation of a mobile world population. It makes little sense to speak about either 'the sovereignty of the local congregation' or 'the solidarity of the episcopate' in such a context. Therefore nothing less than radical renewal will be enough, a renewal as radical as the transformation of the apostolic community into the Church Catholic." [12]

21. Roman Catholic authors recently asserted, "It is impossible to estimate the immense amount of goodness and holiness which

the Reformation, even in what is peculiarly its own, has to offer all Christianity. The Catholic Church cannot do without the Reformation." [13] What can Protestants learn from Roman Catholicism?

22. Is it true today that Protestants are weak in their emphasis on community, while Roman Catholics do not know the Scriptures?

23. Why have Mormons and Jehovah's Witnesses not been accepted into the World Council of Churches? How can we relate to them?

24. The dedication of a Hindu, the gentleness of a Buddhist, the self-surrender of a Muslim, the social concern of a Marxist —are these an indication that Christ is everywhere?

25. Is there such a thing as: Lutheran Faith, Methodist Bible, Roman Catholic Worship, Baptist Baptism, Zen Presbyterianism?

26. In an effort to reverse the fragmentation process in the Christian church a group of British churchmen decided: "It is when a church is truly conscious of the call to mission that it finds division intolerable . . . we need unity for the sake of the world. . . . It is not a question of strategy and logistics. It is rather that as long as the world is confronted by a divided church, the gospel is not presented to it in its fulness, for our disunity obscures the glory of Christ. The world has the right to be confronted with a reconciled and therefore united community of the reconciled. It is too strong for a divided church in that it can use our divisions as an argument or excuse against the acceptance of the Gospel." Is this valid anywhere? If so, how can we proceed in our area to make it a reality? Is it possible to unite in crucial areas such as problems of race or world peace, the care of the elderly, assisting youth, adequate education? Do zoo animals have better facilities than some human beings in our area?

27. If we inhale deeply of its content, this statement may help us today: "If the present social structure were perfect there would be no need for the Church for then the Kingdom of God would be present in its completeness. The Marxist explanation for the continuing existence of religious communities is therefore correct. At least it is correct in this limited but important sense: even in socialist societies a special religious community continues

to exist because, and as long as, the political structure has not yet realized the ultimate form of human life, of true humanity. The mistake of the Marxists is not in the way they characterize the social function of the Churches (or of the religious communities). The Marxist mistake is rather in the illusion that the truly humanistic form of society can be achieved definitely by man, and that it can be achieved in a short historic period." [14]

28. The welfare of future generations may depend on our response to statements such as this: "For the Christian, God has come down into history to transform it from the inside; to the Marxist it seems that belief in God is only an opiate, something that deadens man's concern for the world he must shape. On the practical side, the Christian sees the transcendence of God, and belief in this transcendence, as the condition for the possibility of truly human history, while the Marxist thinks that belief in such transcendence has done little but dull man's sense of creativity in the past. While the latter wants to eliminate this 'drag' of religion, if not religion itself, the former wishes to preserve the Faith, more precisely Faith in Jesus Christ, the Emmanuel God with us, as the only means of humanizing the world. Thus, it is history that draws Christian and Marxist together and it is history that both are trying to affect. . . . Hence, the appropriateness of starting from history in the dialogue between Christians and Marxists. . . . There may be many reproaches you could make to Marxism, but one of the absolutely essential facts that should not fail to impress is that Marxism has given rise to a tremendous energy that has appealed to the working people, people who have been oppressed, people who have been poor, who have been most in need of energy, and it has been doing this now for one hundred years. This is the crucial thing in Marxism. . . . Revolution without dialogue is simply destructive, and not constructive." [15]

"Ernst Bloch, a Marxist, claims that Christianity introduced into the world a category of hope, the notion that real change is possible. Roger Garaudy, another Marxist, says that Christianity unlocked man from his fixed place in the cosmos and made him the agent of historical change. If these men are right, we must concede such notions have gotten lost somewhere over the two millennia of Christian history. Whether or not Christians will reappropriate them remains the crucial question." [16]

29. "The biblical assumption is that what we have is in fact already the one church of Jesus Christ, and that our task is to witness to this reality in terms of structures. If we don't take this latter view, then we have to say that what we do have is not the church but twenty-five culture-communities." [17]

30. Many of the people who ridicule the church would be amazed if they could see the total impact of Christian philanthropy in our day. The record of compassionate giving during our century is a vital part of this story. In spite of all our sins, which are many and serious, the record of giving among some Christians to help people whom they have never seen and who have no claim on them other than being children of the same heavenly Father is encouraging.

Books for Suggested Reading

1. A recent book on Reunion of the Churches.

2. *Wine in Separate Cups,* The Walther League, Chicago, 1967.

3. Marvin T. Judy, *The Cooperative Ministry in Non-Metropolitan Areas.* Abingdon, 1967.

4. Harold E. Fey, *Cooperation in Compassion.* Friendship, 1966.

5. Pierre Berton, *The Comfortable Pew.* Lippincott, 1965.

6. Reuel Howe, *The Miracle of Dialogue.* Seabury, 1962.

7. Wilhelm Pauck, *The Heritage of the Reformation.* Free Press of Glencoe, Inc., 1961.

8. Martin Buber, *I and Thou.* Scribners, 1968.

9. Harvey Cox, ed., *The Church Amid Revolution.* Association, 1967.

10. A. T. Van Leeuwen, *Christianity in World History,* tr. H. H. Hoskins. Scribners, 1964.

11. Herbert Aptheker, ed., *Marxism and Religion.* Humanities Press, 1968.

CHAPTER NINE

INSIDE THE CUP

What produces a reformation?

Unless the Christian church can and will be renewed, it is not worth preserving. But how can this happen?

If we say that "God will do this" or that the Holy Spirit knows when conditions are favorable, then what kind of God have we? Isn't our God always ready and eager for renewal?

Or does it require certain kinds of individuals, i.e. an Ezra, a Luther, a Calvin, a Pope John? Then why were Savonarola and Peter the Great not equally effective?

What are the dynamics of renewal? Is there a syndrome of causes that must be present in order to effect wide and profound changes? Who can break the iron frame of bearded tradition and stifling custom? Commencement speakers may shout, "Keep on growing," but who takes them seriously?

We may read, "But today one could argue with equal cogency that we are witnessing hopeful signs of a renewal and reformation not of Protestantism or of Catholicism, but of the whole Church in all of its great diversity." [1]

What are these hopeful signs? Prerequisite for any change is unrest, frustration, dissatisfaction with the status quo, rebellion. These seem to be experienced today in the cobweb-ridden Vatican and in the air-conditioned headquarters of countless Protestant denominations. Nor is this simply the cry of a few discontented radicals.

History, of course, has recorded many instances of agonizing pleas from reformers who were concerned about specific ills.

Now we must ask another kind of question, "How can we design a system that will continuously reform [i.e. renew] itself, beginning with presently specifiable ills and moving on to ills that we cannot now foresee?" [2]

Applied to the church it seems that two criteria are essential to begin and sustain a stance of renewal.

1. An objective, in-depth study of history, especially of Christian history. Every reformation somehow returned to the fundamentals, the ultimates of our faith, as the final criterion of measurement. Hence one of the hopeful signs in our day is intensive and broad study of the Scriptures and of Christian tradition.

2. A dynamic education whose goal is personal and social responsibility, shifting the burden of pursuing one's own education on those who were confronted by the Gospel. One of the secrets of Luther and Pope John, for instance, was their ability to scatter abroad concerns which were real to them, rather than to hide them in their ivory towers or express them only in heavy, obscure books. Unless someone cares and is sufficiently involved to share his concerns, there will be no reformation. Apathy heals no one.

These two together, and only together, can make for stability in motion, for continuity and change. Impatience with empty forms? Yes. Dissatisfaction with husks? Definitely. But also intensive pursuit of the ultimates which deserve priority and which do not change except in their formulation and a strong program of education.

Even a cursory study of Christian history must reveal the haunting continuity of certain basic aspects of our faith. A few of these were mentioned previously—the centrality of God, concern for man, the acts and words of Jesus Christ, the continuing activity of the Holy Spirit. A few still need to be underscored, for they contribute to the inner renewal of a church which is to go out and serve men.

Worship and Renewal

Endless experiments are being conducted to discover the relevance of meaningful worship. Recall that one of the first acts of Martin Luther was to make available to his contemporaries a worship service which they could understand and in which they could participate. To what degree liturgy or fixed formal services help or hinder has not been determined and may vary with situations and people. But it is one of the hopeful signs that jazz and Bach and chanting and guitars are used today to glorify God in worship.

How could one escape this after paging through the Scriptures? Rather than argue about creation, the ancients praised their Creator. Whole sections of the Bible are poems which these people sang to the glory of God. In fact, one of the most helpful accents of modern Bible studies is the discovery that so much of the Bible is liturgy—that is, expressions of formal worship. Note the subjects some of them chose—Psalm 33, Psalm 92, Psalm 96. Sometimes they heard God speaking to them during their moments of meditation (Isaiah 42:5-8). When their worship became mechanical and perfunctory they heard God's prophetic denunciation (Isaiah 1:11-15; Jeremiah 31:33). The assumption that one can worship and then flout God's commands was attacked by Amos (5:21-24). The right kind of worship must end in witness and stewardship (Psalm 95; Amos 4:4; Deuteronomy 12:6). It was in and for worship that some of the earliest creeds were composed (Deuteronomy 26:5-11; 6:4-9).

Worship is made possible by the condescension of God. This is certainly stressed already in the Old Testament (Exodus 8:22; Deuteronomy 23:14; Psalm 46:5). And the very human saints of that period—Abraham in Egypt, Moses who murdered, David who committed adultery—assure us that we can be ourselves when we worship God and again become the kind of persons God intended us to be by virtue of our creation.

A major contribution of the New Testament in the matter of worship is the addition of sacraments as evidence of Christ's presence with us. Most vividly are we assured of God's love and concern in the Sacraments of Baptism and the Eucharist.

Baptism a Gift

It is treacherous to underscore any one aspect of the Sacraments at the expense of all others. Certainly, they are gifts of a loving Father.

This needs to be said, for infant baptism is under severe attack today. Yet if Baptism is a gift, dare we ask: "Must children be baptized?" We might as well ask, "Must I accept my Christmas gifts?" One never uses the word "must" when a gift is at stake. If Baptism is a gift of God's love, would he not be eager to share this with everyone? Does God love infants?

Yet there is a valid reason for such concerted criticism of infant baptism, since it has so easily become a matter of "cheap grace." Recently a group of young pastors deliberately refused to have their own infants baptized in order to bear testimony to the fact that in church circles Baptism has often become a mere "form." Baptism of one's child may mean suffering and persecution for him, self-sacrifice and ostracism; hence we may wish to walk a bit more slowly to the baptismal font (cf. 2 Timothy 3:12).

For Baptism is a covenant. The nature of this covenant can be compared to a marriage, as in the Book of Hosea or as an adoption by God (1 Peter 2:9). One can become a deserter or a prostitute in this matter.

How God took the initiative and how superior this covenant of Baptism is to the one established in the Old Testament is portrayed graphically in the Epistle to the Hebrews.

Another reason why Baptism has lost some of its appeal may well be the fact that we seldom think of Baptism as a public act. Here God deals with me as an individual, to be sure, and in life's roughest moments I may be able to whisper to myself: "I am baptized"; but we ought to emphasize with equal clarity that Baptism also incorporates me into a community and is at all times the responsibility of the community of love (the church). Because of the mobility of our population, this presents new challenges to every parish.

Another reason why Baptism has lost some of its intrinsic power is that the close relationship between "teach and baptize" has too easily been overlooked. Without instruction Baptism becomes a meaningless rite with superstitious connotations. This emphasis is so strong that a renowned theologian has concluded that we ought never baptize an infant when there is no promise of further instruction, as for instance when it is certain that an infant will not live. Whole portions of the New Testament were written as manuals of instruction for Baptism. Study of these documents is neither a fad nor an option for those who take their Baptism seriously, for there is nothing obscure in Christ's command to "teach and baptize."

The gifts of Baptism may be variously interpreted—forgiveness, adoption, the Holy Spirit, new life—and can always be discussed with profit, provided they lead to mission. In some churches the rite of confirmation is closely associated with Baptism. This has value if meaningful instruction becomes the major thrust and confirmation itself a call to service, like a soldier's induction into an army that is equipped to go out to serve. Present practices in this area are under severe scrutiny.

The Lord's Supper

For further encouragement and strength along the way Christ instituted another sacrament. Strangely enough, he did not explain it in detail. In fact, Christ seldom gave clear and complete answers to questions that were asked of him, a fact which is still a point of dismay to many.

Sometimes he told parables and left the hearer to draw his own conclusions. At other times he countered with a question, "What do you think?" "Which one of you . . . ?"

But once the hearer was involved there was no way of avoiding a decision. Either he came to a new decision concerning himself, his world, and his God or he decided to retain his old views. In either case the thought of his heart was revealed.

There are also many questions about the Lord's Supper which Jesus did not answer. How often shall we commune? How much alcoholic content was in the fluid which Jesus used? Did Judas commune? Must we use one cup or many? If the Lord's Supper is as meaningful as some claim it is, why did Jesus not settle these issues for us?

Our basic decision concerns Christ, who gave this Sacrament. He gave it for the sake of unity. If Holy Communion does not unite, then it should be called unholy communion.

The church has given this sacrament many names: Holy Communion, the Lord's Supper, the Eucharist, the Mass. Instituted by Christ in connection with the Passover, this Sacrament is described in Matthew 26:26-29. While some ignore this Sacrament and others emphasize it at the cost of excluding other gifts of God, we must remember that it is not the Sacrament which saves, but Christ and faith in him. Very much has been written about the Lord's Supper, for while this Sacrament unites in love and fellowship those who receive it, it is also the Sacrament which divides churches and has been the basis of bitter dispute.

Five major assertions concerning the Lord's Supper may well serve as a basis of our discussion and as a source of comfort.

1. The Lord's Supper is a commemoration of a once-and-for-all past event. Every celebration of this meal reminds us of (commemorates) these historical events which can never be repeated, for they happened once and for all time. Participation in this feast always brings us back to the night in which he was betrayed, and therefore it always has the character of a confession.

2. It is a joyful celebration of Christ's real presence and the self-giving of the total Christ. We call it a celebration since it is a joyful moment and not a gloomy experience when Christ comes to us. The concept of sacrifice is also included; Christ gave his life, and our lives are also to be given in the service of love (Romans 12:1).

3. Its effects are both personal and communal. The Lord's Supper is never a private ritual, though I receive its benefits personally. But it is a Sacrament of the church and it unites in fellowship all those who receive Christ here and those who have gone before us in the faith. Where does the liturgy remind us of this? This, of course, also means that it is impossible to wound, injure, or offend any one of our brethren without at the same time offending Christ in him.

4. It is a looking forward to the realization of a full face-to-face fellowship with God. This promise was quite prominent in the thinking of the early church (1 Corinthians 11:26).

5. Christ is the host at this banquet. He extends the invitation and awaits our response. As a baby sitter who confronts a frightened child must win his confidence through kindness and patience, so God comes to us, gives himself, and thus encourages us to accept and to believe. How does the Holy Spirit accomplish this? Such mysteries are not explained.

The Eucharist can easily be perverted if:

1. We mechanize it by assuming that the mere performance of it is all that matters. Traces of this idea meet us already in Paul (1 Corinthians 11:27 ff.).

2. We stress only the differences, the points at issue, among various interpretations. Controversial issues can loom so large that essentials are overlooked. No one knows exactly how Christ is present in the Sacrament. That he comes to me in love is more important than any human speculation.

3. We spiritualize God's great gifts to the exclusion of the physical, or vice versa. This is not an either-or but a both-and. Through plain eating, sin entered the world, and through plain eating Christ comes to us. Hence we ought never take one aspect of Holy Communion and absolutize it, for it is a memorial, a sacrifice, Real Presence, fellowship, thanksgiving. Both are true: "Unless you eat the flesh of the Son of man and drink his blood, you have no life in you" and "It is the spirit that gives life, the flesh is of no avail" (John 5:53, 63a).

4. We forget that the Lord's Supper is a joyous event. This is a celebration of victory. From the beginning the emphasis on joy and thanksgiving was closely associated with this meal. Seriousness and sadness need not be equated. There is some evidence that both the mystery and the joy of Christ's supper are being recaptured in our day.

For Further Discussion

1. Too strong? The Archbishop of Zagreb, Yugoslavia, stated at Vatican II, "The responsibility for modern atheism falls on those Christians who all too stubbornly defend an unchanging social structure while falsely involving the name of God." [3]

2. Does the expression "means of grace" say something meaningful to you?

3. How does this apply to the church: "One of the interesting findings contained in recent research is that the creative individual as a rule chooses to conform in the routine, everyday matters of life, such as speech, dress and manners. One gets the impression that he simply is not prepared to waste his energy

in nonconformity about trifles. He reserves his independence for what really concerns him—the area in which his creative activities occur. This distinguishes him sharply from the exhibitionists who reject convention in those matters that will gain them the most attention." [4]

4. An influential and respected bishop recently resigned in order to work among lepers. What is he saying to you and me?

5. Europe has been called a country of "baptized heathen." Should we limit this to Europe?

6. Which receives more emphasis in your parish, the instruction which precedes or that which follows Baptism? Which one of the Gospels has been called a "manual for adult instruction"? Why?

7. Both of these books are worth reading:

"The act of God in baptism is at the same time an act of Christ. . . . Behind this act of Christ in the present stands his whole ministry from the incarnation to the cross and the resurrection. . . . The question whether baptism is a symbolic act, a 'sign,' or a real act of God is, in view of what we have said here, irrelevant. Baptism is both one and the other. It is not only a symbolic act or a sign. Not even the expression, 'an effective sign,' states clearly what is involved. If we speak of baptism as a sign, it is a sign in the same sense as the works of Christ during his earthly ministry were 'signs.' Baptism is in other words really a divine 'act of power.' " [5]

"It seems entirely possible that an individual was often baptized as a member of an entire household, after a single hearing of the very minimum of 'Gospel,' and only subsequently given detailed instruction. But about the content of the instruction, whenever it was given, there is fortunately more evidence. Even without specific evidence, it would go without saying that, sooner or later, after Baptism if not before, the initial evangelism must be followed by a process of detailed instruction—of 'edification.' And this rearing of the superstructure, this up-building, would, according to the stage at which it occurred, comprise more or less of the basic proclamation, the foundation Gospel." [6]

8. Why is there so much discussion in our day concerning the

rite of confirmation? Does it have a sound biblical basis? Is it wise to suggest a final decision at an early age? Besides Baptism, what other criterion is there for the reception of the Eucharist?

9. On the final page of his book on *The Bondage of the Will* (written at the height of his career in 1525) Luther stated summarily in replying to Erasmus, "I give you hearty praise and commendation on this further account—that you alone, in contrast with all others, have attacked the real thing, that is, the essential issue. You have not wearied me with those extraneous issues about the Papacy, purgatory, indulgences and such like— trifles, rather than issues—in respect of which almost all to date have sought my blood (though without success); you, and you alone, have seen the hinge on which all turns, and aimed for the vital spot." [7] What is this vital spot? Is it still the hinge in our day?

10. "What we need to do is to carry through to a new theological construction on the conviction that the relation between God and his creatures is through and through social. All the traditional doctrines must be reconsidered." [8]

11. Which aspect of the Eucharist should we stress in our day —Christ's presence, our unity, thanksgiving, memorial, sacrifice, mystery? What important element is missing? Is this a good summary of the Lord's Supper:
    a. Christ nourishes us,
    b. Christ becomes one with us,
    c. Christ unites us.

12. What is the background of a special confessional service prior to Communion? Is the practice of your parish in the matter of communing children still valid?

13. Which is better, to receive Holy Communion out of anxiety over sin or out of love for Christ? Why do some people bring the concept of "worthiness" into a discussion of the Lord's Supper? Should we commune as long as one-half of the world's population is starving? (cf. 1 Corinthians 11).

14. Though the lines are not always clearly drawn, this may help us to see some of the major emphases which are divisive in the church today. Ideally, should these be in tension?

Pietism	Servanthood
Bunyan	Bonhoeffer
Religiosity	Holy worldliness
Inner directed	Outer directed
I need thee every hour	Crown him with many crowns
Security	Tension
Gospel then Law	Law then Gospel
Church	Creation
Thinking from above	Thinking from below
Election	Engagement
Orthodox	Dynamic
Denominational	Ecumenical
Bible	God
Proclamation	Education
Tradition	Experimentation
- - - - -	- - - - -
- - - - -	- - - - -

15. Are church buildings necessary? When would disposable buildings be in order? What is your reaction to statements such as this: "The tower of Babel has no top and every temple bears the devastating judgment that it has been 'made by man,'" [9] or: "No structure of church life either in the realm of Church *order* or of church *thought* (theology) can claim eternal validity," or "Just as Christ took form within the changing structures of history, and put on a particular garb, spoke a particular language and related himself to a particular government and particular social problems, so he requires of his people that they take on similar particularity." [10] Is it wise to dismantle the old until we know where we are going?

16. Does God ever work apart from the church? Did Jesus say that the Spirit will convict the church or the world of sin, righteousness, and judgment? What's the difference?

17. The parables deal with cooking, farming, banking, gardening, real estate. Is there a single parable which deals with "religious" matters?

18. Where is the church on Monday morning?

19. "Indeed, all who desire to live a godly life in Christ Jesus

will be persecuted." In what connection did the apostle Paul say this?

20. "With remarkable consistency those who have ministered to the inner-city have discovered that the sacramental character of the community as expressed in the weekly eucharist is essential to the structuring of the Church for mission." [11]

21. What do these statements say to us?

a. "The church at the street corner hides the church Spiritual from view." [12]

b. The church is guilty of "a maximum convergence on areas of minimum need." [13]

c. "Ninety per cent of our church members equate church work with keeping the institutional machinery running. Stewardship (in order to pay for the building) and evangelism (to get more members to share the financial load) are the major fields of mission." [14]

d. Pride (hybris) is an effort to be more than man.

22. We do not fulfill the command "He who has ears to hear, let him hear" (Mark 4:9) simply by making sure that the acoustics are satisfactory. How do we?

23. It was by means of models that Christians explained what they had experienced through faith in Christ. During the Protestant Reformation the favorite model was justification. At other times the models were love, atonement, substitution, satisfaction, redemption, expiation. Is any simple point of departure adequate? What contemporary document uses reconciliation as its favorite model? Which model speaks most meaningfully to you, your neighbor, to a four-year-old, to a university student?

24. What conflict between Peter and Paul is depicted in Galatians 2:11-21? Did they still commune together?

25. Is our concern for structure ever a truly human concern? Was it because of structures that the church shared in the guilt of rendering life inhuman for minority groups? Does our parish give the impression that man has been created for the sake of structure or that structures serve men?

26. What other alternatives are there for the church besides these:

a. To buckle under to all the pressure today to the point where the institutional church will cease to exist.

b. To defend ourselves, rightfully or wrongfully, against all critics and become increasingly irrelevant, putting the wrong corpse into the right coffin.

c. To examine ourselves, discover weaknesses, correct them, develop new approaches, in order to serve our world ever better.

27. The church which only gathers is like salt, clean and white, in a container in the cupboard.

28. Should we or can we recapture the worth of introspection, prayer, silence, contemplation? Need these be artificial and mechanical? Must these concentrate upon the self, or can they be done for the sake of the world?

29. There is much experimentation in our day to discover better forms of worship. Are these worthwhile guidelines? Our forms should be: (a) flexible, (b) relevant, (c) intelligible, (d) ecumenical, (e) scriptural, (f) both communal and personal. Is joy a prominent note in the Christian faith today? Is it possible to celebrate the past, delight in the present, and gratefully anticipate the future without sacrificing one to the other? Is it true that he who never laughs is never serious either?

Books for Suggested Reading

1. *The Church for Others*. World Council of Churches, Geneva, 1967.

2. Thomas Wieser, ed., *Planning for Mission*. World Council of Churches, Geneva, 1966.

3. Gibson Winter, *The Suburban Captivity of the Church*. Doubleday, 1961.

4. Langdon Gilkey, *How the Church Can Minister to the World Without Losing Itself*. Harper, 1964.

5. Monica Furlong, *With Love to the Church*. Hodder and Stoughton, 1967.

6. J. G. Davies, *Worship and Mission*. Association, 1967.

7. Rudolf Otto, *The Idea of the Holy*. Oxford University Press, 1950.

8. Eugene M. Skibbe, *Protestant Agreement on the Lord's Supper*. Augsburg, 1968.

9. John W. Gardner, *Self-Renewal*. Harper, 1963.

10. *One Lord, One Baptism*. Faith and Order Commission, World Council of Churches, SCM, London, 1960.

11. John Jansen. *The Meaning of Baptism*. Westminster, 1958.

CHAPTER TEN

RENEWAL
OF MAN

In some ways major efforts at church renewal center primarily on the renewal of man. No longer is it asserted that saintliness must destroy a person's humanity. "According to the Protestant principle there is no Spirituality which is based on the negation of matter, because God as Creator is equally near the material and the spiritual. Matter belongs to the good creation, and its humanist affirmation does not contradict Spirituality." [1]

In fact, objective study of the Scriptures has revealed anew that one measure of a healthy faith is its ability to face the threatening aspects of reality without succumbing to fear, hostility, or anxiety. An unhealthy faith runs away from life and becomes obsessed with a portion in order to avoid the whole. That is, the body may be denied for the soul's sake, or the future becomes so all-absorbing as to blot out the present, or all truth is limited to a personal interpretation of the Bible. A healthy faith unites existence; an unhealthy faith divides it. This attempt to affirm creation is one of the most wholesome discoveries of contemporary Bible study.

Affirmation of Creation

Today's affirmation of creation has assumed many aspects and can be discussed from many angles. In some ways this is a return to the Old Testament unity of mind and body. Such an emphasis may include a scriptural frankness about sex and may lead to a profound theology of eroticism wherein sexuality

95

will take its place as a joyful gift of God, experienced with the frank joyfulness of the Song of Songs. In a way this is an attempt to recover all those dimensions which have been consigned to the "non-spiritual." It will be difficult to learn once again that grace does not destroy nature but rather fulfills it—in fact, this may be the most crucial issue confronting our generation. Man and nature together constitute our world—flawed by sin, subject to time, but open toward grace. The world is never simply a good thing or a bad thing but a good thing spoiled, always a God-haunted house. "Without the Gospel the world is without sense; without the world, the Gospel is without reality." [2]

Among the leaders of this movement is a theologian and paleontologist who died almost unnoticed in 1955. Since then some two thousand books have been written about him and literally thousands of articles. Study groups have been organized universally to attest to his phenomenal influence in our time.

The writings of Teilhard de Chardin are too involved and profound for review here. What is most alluring in his work is the wonderful prospect of a total and aggregate perspective of the whole universe in which matter and spirit, body and soul, nature and the supernatural, science and faith, will find their unity in Christ. His emphasis on the cosmic, global dimensions of Christ's work reminds one of Chapter 1 of Colossians. Because of the happy combination of scientific expertise and Christian commitment in his writings he was able to develop a world view which finds ready echo in the minds of modern man. A refreshing appreciation and affirmation of creation permeates all that he offers, though a recognition of evil and the demonic is not always apparent.

Life Together

Concomitant with a wholesome emphasis on creation comes a new appreciation of man as a collective being. If Teilhard has helped us in the former, then Dietrich Bonhoeffer has assisted greatly in clarifying for us the latter. The shape of our community, our life together, he maintained, is a shape open to empirical analysis and diagnosis. Since his day sociologists have carried out such empirical investigation of the relationship between religion and society, often with devastating results. At least these studies provide a warning that religion tends to be transformed by culture. Their efforts seem to indicate that groups are not always entities with a system of ethics but only with an ethos, so that it is individuals that usually supply the prophetic protest and the catalytic initiative toward reformation of the group.

This may force us to face moral issues with a new appreciation of their complexity and a new stress on their social dimensions. If we take into account the area of man's collective behavior—i.e., his use and misuse of economic and political power, his responses because of race or nationality—we discover that morality is seldom private. How can we answer today the question: "Who is my neighbor?" in an employee society where life is impersonalistic?

Mutual Ministry

Within the confines of the church one of the most radical and far-reaching changes affecting almost every area of its life is a scintillating and provocative emphasis on the "laity." It has been stated, "The recovery of this laos-consciousness, with the rediscovery of the role of the laity in the life and mission of the Church, is the heart of church renewal in our time." [3] The New Testament word "laos" was given a faulty interpretation for years. We assumed that laity referred to the non-ordained, when originally it referred to the people of God.

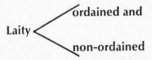

Hence the word "laity" is most misleading unless we accompany the use of this word with an explanation. In the church all have a ministry and all are to be equipped for such service.

To put this doctrine of the mutual ministry or the priesthood of believers into action in parish life is a long-range effort. Until progress has been made, it may only accentuate the problem of what the ordained ministry is all about. If all are to minister, then why have a salaried, ordained pastor? He becomes a teacher of ministers. In the eyes of some this will make him a revolutionary.

If our fundamental affirmation in this area is that the non-ordained (laity) are being thrust into the foreground as interpreters of the Christian faith to a skeptic public, if this servant-hood of our people is the major approach of the church to an emerging society, then this poses the task of lay training as the defining characteristic of the professional ministry. Such claims that Christian people become engaged in ministry will necessitate breaking through existing forms and may subject the pastor not only to attacks from his own constituency but also to criticism from his organizational superiors. This is the risk which confronts many parishes today.

Such efforts at renewal do not ask mainly whether the existence of the church is justified. If Christ has commissioned the church to a task, then it is justified and meaningful. Our question is a practical one—how the church can best fulfill her commission in our milieu. "Although the nature of the Church is of divine origin and indestructible, nevertheless its realization in everyday life, even when under the protection of the promised Holy Ghost, is still exposed to man's freedom, to his whims and to his errors." [4]

The need today seems to be not primarily a new doctrine of ministry but a rediscovery of the prophetic nature of ministry. How are Christians to be faithful to God's Word and relevant to God's world at the same time? How can we express the priestly "yes" through worship and witness and also the prophetic "no" through love seeking justice? If in the past one of our problems has been a clericalism which frustrated the ministry of the laity, how can we today affirm creation and the world as the arena for Christian ethical service? While we tend to complain about the impersonal structures of power and economics in modern society —they are basically morally neutral—how can we help them to be agencies for good? How are we assisting in the search for new ways of loving our neighbor?

In an affluent society such as ours this will require a much greater emphasis on giving. Both human need and God's love are basic motives for giving.

Dynamic Education

Much of the above is so new for us—and all of it has become so complex—that we need a much stronger emphasis on a dynamic kind of Christian education.

One of the newer emphases will be a change in the method of communicating the Gospel. "The educational function of the church does not consist in information about the history and the doctrinal self-expressions of the church. A confirmation-instruction which does merely that misses its purpose, although it may communicate useful knowledge. Neither does the educational function of the church consist in the awakening of a subjective piety, which may be called conversion but which usually disappears with its emotional causation. A religious education which tries to do this is not in line with the educational function of the church. The church's task is to introduce each new generation into the reality of the Spiritual Community, into its faith and into its love. This happens through participation in degrees of maturity, and it happens through interpretation in degrees of understanding. There is no understanding of a church's life without participation; but without understanding the participation becomes mechanical and compulsory." [5]

In some ways the changes in communicating the Gospel call for radical study of our structures and approaches. This is underscored especially by those who view the "sermon" type of communication as rather useless. Why this methodic attack on a time-honored way of transmitting the Gospel? "The present state of the church's preaching strikingly discloses the extremity of its present need, wherein it can only pray, with unembellished fervor: 'Come, Creator Spirit.' " [6] "The clergyman must become a prophet and engage the congregation in dialogue." [7] Quite a change in emphasis is indicated when we are told not to think "that pastoral counseling is always related to people in trouble and is something quite different from teaching or evangelism." [8] "The professional ministry will no longer be able to understand itself as primarily a preaching, pastoral, and sacramental ministry, but will have to become primarily and self-consciously a theological-educational ministry." [9] "The mission of the Christian is the way of love . . . we have spent too much time simply talking." [10] In a popular magazine David Edwards argues "that preaching is on the way out, and that in the future the Word of God will be expressed by dialogue rather than monologue, instead of sermons, study-group discussions between ministers and laymen." [11] This may be stated in extreme form in order to awaken us to the need for dialogue and involvement.

For Further Discussion

1. Luther expressed the hope that the time may come when the congregation would defend the Scripture against the preacher. Has that day arrived?

2. The translation of Ephesians 4:11-12 is more correct in the New English Bible—"to equip God's people for work in his service," than in the Revised Standard Version, "for the equipment of the saints, for the work of ministry." What's the difference?

3. Max Weber wrote: "The idea of duty in one's calling prowls about in our lives like the ghost of dead religious beliefs." Was he right?

4. Of what statement by Christ does the quotation by Tillich offered above remind you? What does Acts 8 say about the unordained in the early church?

5. Can a sermon be dialogue? How?

6. In his provocative book *The Church Inside Out*, Johannes C. Hoekendijk suggests that a modern catechism would have to "lead us on a course of thinking things through with question after question after question, thus inviting us to search things out for ourselves." [12] Is the Christian faith worth asking questions about? Do daily Bible readings help in this?

7. What does this say to you: "Prophecy without involvement is for the birds." Do we know without participation? Do Luke 11:52 and Matthew 23:13 refer to this?

8. Why are so many altars placed in the center of church buildings again?

9. Have you found any value in retreats? Why or why not?

10. What does it mean that I must first be able to love myself before I can love someone else?

11. What implications arise from this statement: "As soon as man has been understood as man-before-God (the encounter) confusion about the nature of the ministry has begun to disappear." [13]

12. Does this help to clarify what we are trying to say: "The Christianity that conquered the Roman Empire was not an affair of brilliant preachers addressing packed congregations. We have, so far as I know, nothing much in the way of brilliant preachers in the first three hundred years of the church's life. . . . The great preachers came after Constantine the Great; and before that Christianity had already done its work and made its way right through the Empire from end to end. When we try to picture how it was done, we seem to see domestic servants teaching Christ in and through their domestic service, workers doing it through their work, small shopkeepers through their trade, and so on rather than eloquent propagandists swaying mass meetings of interested inquirers." [14]

13. Why is it sometimes maintained that "Baptism is ordination"?

14. Is it true that the Christian ethic is a faith rather than a love ethic? Or should we call it an ethic of thanksgiving? If what is starkly unique about the Christian ethic is Christ, then is the major emphasis on inwardness, solitary behavior, or on neighborly conduct and brotherly concern? Why did Jesus frequently use the word "must" in ethical matters? "I must work the works of him that sent me," "I must preach the kingdom to other cities also," "I must abide in your house."

15. If this is true, then what should be our reaction? "The largest amount of the church dollar is spent on the maintenance, repair, and renovation of old buildings and the construction of new ones. . . . It is easier for a camel to pass through the eye of a needle than for a financially secure and morally self-satisfied Church to enter the kingdom of heaven." [15]

16. A group of church men after struggling with questions of morality came to this conclusion: "Unless a deliberate attempt is to be made by society, acting through the agency of the law, to equate the sphere of crime with that of sin, there must remain a realm of private morality which is, in brief and crude terms, not the law's business. To say this is not to condone or encourage private immorality. . . . . It is not the business of the state to intervene in the purely private sphere but to act solely as the defender of the common good . . . Sin as such is not the

concern of the state, but affects the relations between the soul and God. Attempts by the state to enlarge its authority and invade the individual conscience, however high-minded, always fail and frequently do positive harm." [16] Fornication and adultery are outlawed under sodomy statutes in the United States but are legal in England. Who is right?

17. "I will be the first to admit and concede, as I think all theologians would today, that the Biblical tradition, the Judeo-Christian tradition, has become infected by a basically foreign distrust of the body, of the world, of the things of this earth. Any kind of prophet, whether he be within or without the fold, who criticizes the Judeo-Christian tradition for this heresy, is welcome. . . . I think we need to discover once again that sexuality means intimacy. And intimacy is something which only two persons who know something about each other *alone* can develop. . . . The whole question of developing and understanding sexual intimacy in our time is closely related to the need which all of us have to discover: our own identities. . . . Therefore, the real issue is not whether or not you have intercourse before you're married. The real issue is whether or not you are willing to take the risk of understanding sexuality . . . will it be authentic intimacy?" [17]

18. A wife discovers that her husband is involved in an illicit affair with another woman. Would she be satisfied if he promised her that he would gradually taper off this relationship during the next ten years? A man in prison is informed that the court has discovered he is innocent. Would he be satisfied if the warden assured him that he would be granted full freedom in ten years with free Sundays in the meantime? Is this a valid parable of the usual treatment given to minority groups? Are freedom and power at the center of the Gospel?

19. The scientific revolution "outshines everything since the rise of Christianity and reduces the Renaissance and Reformation to the rank of . . . mere internal displacements. . . . It changed the character of men's habitual mental operation." [18]

20. "The whole creation is on tiptoe to see the wonderful sight of the sons of God coming into their own" (Romans 8:19).

Books for Suggested Reading

1. James D. Smart, *The Rebirth of Ministry.* Westminster, 1960.

2. Dietrich Bonhoeffer, *Life Together,* tr. John Doberstein. Harper, 1954.

3. Elma Greenwood, *How Churches Fight Poverty.* Friendship, 1967.

4. Hiley H. Ward, *Creative Giving.* Macmillan, 1958.

5. Harvey Cox, *The Secular City.* Macmillan, 1965.

6. Robert Raines, *New Life in the Church.* Harper, 1961.

7. Nels F. S. Ferré, *A Theology for Christian Education.* Westminster, 1967.

8. Gerhard Lenski, *The Religious Factor.* Doubleday, 1961.

9. Michael H. Murray, *The Thought of Teilhard de Chardin.* Seabury, 1966.

10. Joseph Sittler, *The Care of the Earth.* Fortress, 1964.

CHAPTER ELEVEN

CAPITULATION
OR REVOLUTION?

The statements are largely negative, but one cannot escape them in our day, namely that the church has little to offer in the area of definite beliefs and especially in the sphere of morals. Permissiveness is the trend; no standard of conduct is the order of the day. Mores are changing so rapidly that most of us are bewildered by the swiftness with which old restraints are losing their force.

These new postures alarm many concerned citizens, especially sociologists and Christians. Hedonism invariably leads to decay.

Certainly the climate of candor and openness is not to be negated and will probably not reverse itself. We shall have to learn to live with a degree of candor and freedom much greater than any we have had for centuries.

If it is true that all the old codes have broken down, is there nothing left? Has the Christian Gospel no contribution to offer in this dilemma? To strip away sham and cant is wholesome, but is there no right and wrong? If there are no tiny absolutes, are there big ones? If the stress is on humanization, how can this be accomplished?

New Morality

Since many of the changes have become most apparent in the area of Christian ethics, the whole movement has sometimes been dubbed simply "the New Morality," or "contextual ethics."

The expression was first used as a derogatory term by the Supreme Congregation of the Roman Catholic Church in Rome in 1956 when this group feared that the more dynamic approach would justify artificial birth control. Since then both pros and cons have received considerable attention and produced a goodly share of confusion.

It would be a pity if the slick pronouncement that the New Morality is "the old immorality condoned" should retain currency, especially if this were to lead to the only possible alternative of a return to legalistic morality. At the other extreme we find such statements as, "What we see in the new morality is the church catching up with Christianity." [1]

There is no question about it, the New Morality makes ethical decisions much more difficult and agonizing. Whether it leads to lack of restraint and immoral conduct can be debated. If to be "moral" means to be capable of being influenced by a sense of right, then the new morality is not primarily new, though its tenets and approaches may be new for us.

A few general principles seem to have jelled by now.

1. The New Morality promotes, or at least accepts, an increasing rejection of authority. To go on emphasizing the importance of adhering to authoritative standards in an age when both the authority and the standards are suspect is to invite attention only from the aged. Few parents still insist on an authoritarian approach in the home. Is this good or bad? One of the difficulties today of an authoritarian ethic in the church is that not only the very authority is questioned but also the various interpretations promulgated by different individuals and groups.

2. The New Morality is also characterized by an empirical approach to all questions. The question applied in almost every instance is: Will it work? "The central question, then, seems to be not what religion is, and certainly not what 'religious truth' might be, but what religion has done for men and what it might do for men today." [2]

3. Possibly the most discerning feature of the New Morality is the basic presupposition that all decisions are to be intensely personal. How does my answer affect human beings? Christ did not offer long dissertations on love; he simply practiced it. We

are not interested in a metaphysical discussion of justice. Our duty and privilege is to engage in acts of justice. "Anything is lawful if it helps" (1 Corinthians 6:12). When Christ was asked: "Who is my neighbor?" he did not answer with an absolute principle but with a living situation. Is it not true that persons are more valuable, immeasurably more valuable, than principles? "Have you never read what David did, when he was . . . hungry, he and those who were with him: how he entered the house of God . . . and ate the bread of the Presence, which it is not lawful for any but the priests to eat, and also gave it to those who were with him?" (Mark 2:25 f.).

4. A fourth thesis of the New Morality is an emphasis on the situation or context. More and more we are coming to a consensus that there is more than one way to look at any problem and that whether an answer is true or false depends upon the particular point of reference. The only absolute is love for neighbor.

If morality cannot be governed by codes or commandments, then how does one make ethical decisions? Not by some absolute, timeless code but by love. One starts with the person rather than with principles, with experience rather than with authority, with freedom rather than fixity. The degree of awareness, the degree of love present, is more determinative, more complex, more compassionate, and more convincing than the codes applied by self-styled moralists. This does not mean that respect for law has been discarded. "There is no question that law has its place, but that place is at the boundaries and not at the center"; this summarizes the newer view of the law. "The deeper one's concern for persons, the more effectively one wants to see love buttressed by law." [3]

Again it will have to be underscored that love (agape) is the most searching and demanding criterion and motive for any and all ethical acts. Law is a guideline—otherwise every decision we make would have to start from scratch—but the ultimate and decisive factor is not law but love, according to Christ's summary of the law. Some advocate that it would be better to ask: What is the most fellowship-creating thing to do? Dietrich Bonhoeffer made the cryptic statement, "The guilt may often lie with the community rather than with the individual." [4]

What a tremendous burden this throws on the educational program of the church is immediately apparent. Training people to make mature decisions will be a long and arduous process. And any suggestion that the new approach is a concession to the indulgences of a soft society is not only far from the truth but also ignores this effort at training for maturity. The whole educational and communal and religious life will have to be geared toward helping people to face decisions in their lives from the viewpoint: What does love require? Now that this has happened, what can I do? This is far from a cavalier attitude toward ethical decision, but it does remind us that ethics will be controlled by the freedom of Christian men and women.

This approach ought also help us (though no one has found the final solution) to find a common moral ground between Christians and non-Christians. Because of factors which need not be rehearsed here we are increasingly becoming one world. Hence we dare not confront our generation with an ethic which applies only to the Christian. Love is a relationship among people, valid wherever people are present.

Sex and Marriage

In some ways the newer emphases have been especially apparent in the area of sexuality, at least in popular discussion.

A Christian has first to remind himself in no uncertain terms that the Christian view of sex and marriage is not a theology of the marriage ceremony. How this emphasis developed is not our concern here, but in the minds of many the ceremony seemed to be basic. A man and a woman marry each other when their mutual consent is the response to each other and the acceptance of responsibility for each other. The ceremony is of significance only for functional reasons, as a kind of announcement to the community that they will be responsible to each other. Legalities and ceremonies simply exhibit to others the fact that these two are married. The Christian responsibility now on our part is to assist them to be loyal and loving toward each other. Sexual intercourse is then the consummation of an existing marriage, and traditionally this was reserved until after the ceremony had been held.

In this connection a thorough study by Quakers asked, "When is it right for intercourse to take place," and answered, "It should *not* happen until the partners come to know each other so well that the sexual contact becomes a consummation, a deeply meaningful total expression of a friendship in which each has accepted the other's reality and shared the other's interests." Positively they add, "At once we are aware that this is to ask for nothing less than the full commitment of marriage, indeed most marriages begin with a much less adequate basis." [5]

Does not all this leave a "twilight zone" where no rules seem to apply? Certainly, but rules and commandments have loopholes also. The strength of this is that it attempts to place responsibility where it belongs. As the Friends add, "Where there is genuine tenderness, an openness to responsibility, and the seed of commitment, God is surely not shut out. Can we not say that God can enter any relationship in which there is a measure of selfless love?" [6]

Does this make the sexual love-act as casual a gesture as a kiss, as has been charged? That seems to be a misinterpretation of every emphasis on responsible and loving action. No matter how great the revolution may be the Christian Gospel does not advocate free and irresponsible acts. It does put love at the center as the basic and ultimate motivating force. Traditional codes and efforts probably aimed at this as much as the New Morality does. We should be grateful that love is simply underscored doubly in our day.

Christ and Culture

In all of this the danger is extremely acute that we will simply follow cultural dictates and hallow them with Gospel imperatives. No one has found the ultimate solution as far as a Christian social outlook is concerned. Traditionally three types have been developed roughly as follows:

1. Christ above Culture (Roman Catholic)
2. Christ and Culture in Paradox (Lutheran and Greek Orthodox)
3. Christ Transforming Culture (Augustine and Calvin)

The question remains: Are these to be synthesized, are they incompatible, are they complementary, should they serve as correctives to each other, or is a sterile antagonism the only possibility?

Whether in morals or politics or economics, the easy way out is for the church to capitulate to culture. But World War II— with its sad illustrations of churches which submitted to national pride and pressure—has awakened many in the church to the fact that we are not here simply to capitulate to majority vote. While the "remnant" is sometimes extolled as the quiet in the land, there were also prophetic voices in the past who rebelled against injustice and discrimination. In that sense Christ himself was a rebel of the first order.

Hence a good deal of attention is being given in our day to a theology of revolution, not as though this were a strangely new system of beliefs, though it does accent an aspect of the Gospel which had been pushed into the background. Bonhoeffer, Niemoeller, and Lilje are honored because they dared to oppose a ruthless dictator. When and where should we encourage revolution today? If a dictator is the cause of much suffering, have we a moral responsibility to interfere? Luther encouraged active resistance to the emperor, and Calvin had considerable trouble with political superiors. There are few things more tragic than a man or a nation sleeping through a revolution.

For Further Discussion

1. Why could Luther say: "Every man ought to write his own Ten Commandments"?

2. History offers many examples of how the views of the church have changed—capital punishment, hanging for theft, status of women, slavery, usury, birth control. How can this be if truth never changes? What does not change? What changes may come soon?

3. Why is there less and less censorship of films and books?

4. Is it true on the basis of the Gospel that "charity is more important than chastity"?

5. We are just beginning to discover what morality is all about It is concerned with how we behave toward one another and not how much of our bodies we happen to display. Would you agree?

6. Which is closer to pornography: the picture of a near-nude body or the photo of a policeman deliberately backing his horse over a colored youth? Which word is more obscene—a four-letter word or "nigger"?

7. We used to have clear "yes and no" answers to different problems. Why not now?

8. Discuss: Christian education does not consist of persuasion but of confrontation. The ultimate goal of education is to shift to the individual the burden of pursuing his own education. Is it possible to teach without manipulating the student? When does our discussion become human engineering, when is it mere information, when is it a call to commitment?

9. Do you agree: "A person is being educated in the sense of adult education if he tries continuously to understand himself, society, and the world, and then to act in accordance with this understanding"? [7]

10. How would you answer the following criticism of the New Morality:

a. It ignores the fact that we have a history or a tradition.

b. This exchanges a tyranny of contemporary prejudice for a tyranny of tradition, or a conformity of relativistic ethos for a conformity of legalism.

c. The commandments are difficult to apply today, but are these not also weasel words: love, maturity, responsibility (to whom?)?

11. If both sexes are important, then why is our image of God masculine?

12. The *Playboy* philosophy states that any act of love-making, especially sexually, is moral if it does not hurt anyone, whereas the Christian principle is that no sexual act, whether homo or auto or hetero, is moral unless it helps someone. Right?

13. This has been used as an expression of the fact that faith ought to make us whole: "I came into the church I used to go to as a child and found my girl there. We embraced and the most powerful feeling filled me—of being in touch with life's mys-

tery. Just then some elders appeared and frowned a forbidding 'No!' at our embrace."

14. Would you say that the debates between the "old" and "new" morality are fruitless and confused? Is it too simple to describe the old and new tensions as between legalistic and compassionate approaches to problems of human conduct? Is there enough validity in this distinction to make us restudy our ethical decisions? What does it mean that Christ calls us to a relationship?

15. What loopholes as far as the commandments are concerned exasperate you?

16. Would you agree that the premise in this statement is true, while the conclusion is debatable? "Well aware of the disasters created by preaching the Law only, ministers tend to say more about the Gospel. . . . But in the long run this has the effect of undermining the Law itself, at least in so far as the Law must be spelled out as a specific guide to conduct." [8]

17. Can a couple say, "We shall do as we please and what we do is no one else's business"? Can love ever say, "This is no one else's business"? Does love have a "built-in moral compass"?

18. Is this statement still true? If so, how should we react? "By a careful survey of readily available social facts we demonstrated conclusively that the theory that the modern family has lost its functions is one of the greatest academic illusions of our century, if indeed it is not *the greatest* academic illusion." [9]

19. Is it correct to say that Jesus' parables and teachings and acts are illustrations of what love may require in a particular situation?

20. Are shotgun marriages advisable just to legitimize a child?

21. What did these Reformers mean with such pregnant statements as: Luther—"through love being changed into each other" or Calvin—"let us be whatever we are for each other"?

22. How would you answer the question: Is the girl who gives her chastity for her country's welfare any less honorable than the boy who gives his leg?

23. In a recent film a prostitute picked up a young sailor who was in deep distress over his incapacity to perform an act of sexual intercourse. The prostitute gave herself to him in such a way that he acquired confidence and self-respect. Would you say that this was a promiscuous sexual act?

24. When did the sexual revolution begin? In 1721 Harvard undergraduates formally debated the question: "Whether it be fornication to lie with one's sweetheart before marriage."

25. Situation ethics requires that one approach a moral decision fully armed with the ethical maxims of one's heritage and fellowship. Is this possible? How?

26. If our discussions are not correlated with reality, they not only lack reality but are hardly meaningful. Truth always deals with situations and decisions. Did this chapter confront us with any valid choices?

27. How would you answer youth who claim: The church is a religious chain-store doling out packaged worship, packaged comfort, packaged doctrine? How old was Jesus when he said, "He that has seen me has seen the Father"? Which is more difficult: for youth to listen to the church or for the church to listen to youth? Today's parents were concerned about personal morality such as sex, the proper use of money and of time, but they were very tolerant in their social ethics, permitting economic exploitation, war, and racial injustice. Today's youth tends to be concerned about social ethics, especially race relations and war, but show great tolerance in personal matters such as sex and the use of money and time.

28. Are there any old customs which may still have value? Do we have any icons? Would fasting be a good custom if it reminded us of all the people who are hungry?

29. What is meant by the "ladder" or "spiral" emphasis in Christian ethics? How do you react to the following: "If we want to attain true humility and come quickly to the top of that heavenly ascent to which we can only mount by lowliness in this present life, we must ascend by good works, and erect the

mystical ladder of Jacob, where angels ascending and descending appeared to him"?[10]

30. What is the difference between Christian ethics and moralism?

31. "We live in an age in which man is demonstrating that he can do almost anything. This is as it should be, if he is truly created in God's image. But it also means that he needs ethics more than ever. For the man who can do almost anything is more hard put to decide *what* to do than the man who cannot do very much in any case." [11]

32. Have you experienced the following?

a. The more you ask about God's will the more you discover you do not know. The more you do the will of God the more you realize you do not want to do it. Read Luke 14:28-33.

b. Man's favorite idolatry is to have a private God.

33. What religious clichés weary you? Do you know what is meant when someone asks you to "follow the Christian way of life"?

34. If Christ invites all people, is it pure arrogance for any congregation to vote on the question as to who can join?

35. When visited by a young pastor Mr. A asked, "Do you want me to come to your church Sunday mornings? For years now my wife and I have taken several kids from the slums into the hills for the weekend. We take them skating and swimming, fill them with good food, and return them to their homes on Sunday evening. Do you want us to drop this so that we can sit in your church for an hour on Sunday morning?" What would you have answered?

36. Some people decry the commercialism of Christmas and Easter. At least this gives some needy people added income. What could we do about these festivals that would be helpful?

37. Jesus maintained, "He that is not for me is against me." Where is the line of demarcation? Is a part of me always against him, always for him?

38. Are you a revolutionary? Why? Why not? When do you

not only protest but even oppose a government? To what degree are we guilty of the death of soldiers and civilians in other countries? Why do we help to crush revolutions in other parts of the world? "The prospects for reform in the institutional Church leave many of us bored. At the present moment, the real and worthwhile problem is how to understand, and how to assist, the serious revolution occurring in the United States." [12]

39. Were the following guilty of civil disobedience—Peter, Bunyan, Gandhi, Washington, Hamilton, Jefferson, Bonhoeffer, Niemoeller, King, Coffin? Should church buildings again become "sanctuaries for conscience"? What is Arthur I. Waskow saying about creative policies of disorder, or Richard J. Neuhaus about the church and politics?

40. What's the difference between saying: "You ought to love" and Matthew 22:37-39? Why could Augustine say: "Love and do what you will"? Did he? Do the commandments seem like an expression of God's love to you? Why are we afraid to love?

41. There are sharp statements in the Bible against homosexuals (such as in Genesis 19 and Romans 1). Were these people possibly incapable of normal sexual relations?

42. The number of children a couple desires is entirely their own responsibility. Right? Is it right for a state to pass laws on sterilization, or on euthanasia?

43. Why is it dangerous to make a list of sins? Which sins are more subtle: sins of omission or sins of commission?

44. Even if Christ's name is not mentioned or known, when reconciliation occurs is he present?

45. Is there any value in group confession?

46. How would you answer these old favorites: How does Christ set us free? From what has Christ set us free? For what has Christ set us free? In what way is God free?

47. The church is Peter walking on the water. If it looks out for itself it sinks.

48. What is your reaction to the following: What is the pur-

pose of laws and codes? "They were added," according to Paul, "because of sin." Any person who has the mind of Christ can be trusted to do God's will without having exact rules spelled out for him. In fact, he may in particular instances find it necessary to violate a code or a system in order to do his Father's will. But the person who does not sense his responsibility to Christ will misuse this freedom and become a menace to himself and others. Even for Christians it is hard to draw a line between freedom and responsibility. Here the church can help by providing guidelines for Christian consciences. Since they are guidelines, they do not permit us to pass judgment on others who decide differently. Guidelines may even change as situations change through the years. The church should not presume to speak for or to those who do not belong to her fellowship. Certainly the church should not pass laws, for this is not her peculiar gift. The church's best and peculiar gift is the Gospel.

49. In reference to the care of the earth Dr. Joseph Sittler asks: "Can the spirit that won a continent sustain a national society? . . . We have fashioned a society and an industrial order at the cost of polluting water, befouling our air, scarring our land, besmirching the beautiful, clogging and confusing our living space. We have managed all human placement and means of movement for our convenience as consumers, not for our dignity as human beings." [13]

50. "Mark 11:15-17. The implication seems to be that our Lord did not approve of selling things as a religious enterprise and that He forcefully discouraged those who tried to do it. This is somewhat misleading. It was the duty of the temple worshiper to offer sacrifices. And sacrificial pigeons were an appropriate commodity for sale. The real objection lies elsewhere. In fact, Jesus was actually fighting for the outsider. The sales counters had been set up in the outer courtyard of the temple, the very place where the Gentile, the outsider, was allowed to worship. Our Lord objected to the noise and traffic in this witness area. Thus he indignantly reminded those whom he chastised: 'Is it not written, my house shall be called a house of prayer for all nations?' And this is a frightening reminder to the church that the real thing which made Jesus angry was the setting up of

barriers against the outsider. The scriptural base is the right place to start understanding stewardship. When we start there we are led into, not away from, total involvement in creation." [14]

51. Luther once said that as Christians we must every day anew "creep into the cross of our vocation" by being fully what we are—young or old, married or unmarried, a master or a servant. Our everyday life is our cross. By taking up the cross and by risking the pain of living wholly in this world we become true Christians. Would this make us "contagiously human"?

52. "A civil law should be broken if the lawbreaker considers it unjust." [15]

53. Statements such as the following are popular today. What is your reaction?

a. "All theology is ethics."

b. "Ethics is aesthetics."

c. "The unique commodity of the church is ethics."

d. "Suddenly a theological ethic which tries to arrive at solutions on the basis of well defined traditions of grace and law seems irrelevant."

e. "What God requires does not change, but the context of life has changed."

54. Is this a good way to put it? "The difference between believers and unbelievers, both of whom are involved in the new humanity, is rather the difference between being in a situation which is hidden and being in one which is open." "A koinonia ethic is concerned with relations and functions, not with principles and precepts." "Calvin regarded the sexual act as 'undefiled, honorable and holy because it is a pure institution of God,' it is the devil who leads us to imagine 'that we are polluted by intercourse.' " [16]

55. "The way a man looks at his neighbor or talks to a child, the way he eats, walks, or shakes hands, or the way in which a group behaves toward minorities is more expressive of faith and love than any stated belief." [17]

56. What problems remain for us in Christian ethics which are peculiar to our situation?

Books for Suggested Reading

1. J. C. Hoekendijk, *The Church Inside Out*. Westminster, 1966.

2. James H. Burtness, *Whatever You Do*. Augsburg, 1967.

3. Joseph Fletcher, *Situation Ethics*. Westminster, 1956.

4. Erich Fromm, *The Heart of Man*. Harper, 1965.

5. J. A. T. Robinson, *Christian Morals Today*. Westminster, 1964.

6. Paul Lehmann, *Ethics in a Christian Context*. Harper, 1963.

7. Reinhold Niebuhr, *An Interpretation of Christian Ethics*. Harper, 1935.

8. Sherwin Bailey, *Common Sense about Sexual Ethics*. Macmillan, 1962.

9. Simon Doniger, ed., *Sex and Religion Today*. Association Press, New York, 1953, esp. pp. 178 ff.

10. Paul Ramsey, *Deeds and Rules in Christian Ethics*. Scribner, 1967.

11. Martin Luther, "Sermon on Good Works," Holman Edition, Vol. I. Muhlenberg (Fortress), 1943.

12. John Calvin, *Institutes of Christian Religion*. Book III, tr. John Allen. Westminster, 1936.

13. John C. Bennett *et al.*, *Storm Over Ethics*. United Church Press, 1967.

14. Emil Brunner, *The Divine Imperative*. Westminster, 1947.

CHAPTER TWELVE

ANATOMY OF FUTILITY

There is a good kind of trouble and a bad kind. Whether our present problems are of the former or latter kind remains to be seen. Can riots and hatreds and cleavages and wars produce good? Is it possible to move from deception, unawareness, cynicism, and despair toward honesty, awareness, freedom, trust, and loving concern? Where there is danger the good also grows, and where the good grows there danger thrives also. To abandon ourselves and all meaning has value only if there is a prospect of something better.

Futility follows its own indigenous patterns. Certainly one of these is a false harping on sin.

Fortunately, one of the more subtle changes among the newer approaches is the church's response to the problem of sin. It is an extremely acute issue—not that we have to prove the presence or even the horror of sin—and we need to consider how to deal with it. Christianity has been accused of being essentially a guilt-producing religion. The kind of emphasis on sin which the church often proclaims, it is charged, merely perpetuates a fictitious kind of guilt and enables the church to keep lower classes in submission. "The more guilty one feels, the more easily one submits because the authority has proven its power by its right to accuse. . . . Guilt is . . . in a genuine moral sense self-mutilation"[1]

Already Dietrich Bonhoeffer warned against a similar tendency of "believing in sin," that is, in always finding some sin as the starting point for preaching the Gospel. Such a procedure easily produces fictitious sin.[2]

Sin has been defined in many ways. Buddhism considers it misconduct that one can correct by one's own efforts. For Islam it is a transgression of natural law. For humanism sin is an offense against man. For Marx it is an imperfect cog in the wheel of human progressive evolution. For Christians it is a refusal of God's love in Christ. Always sin is a violation of love.

Hence it may not be necessary in our day to convince people that they are sinful as much as to offer help out of their predicament. "It is not the consciousness of sin," maintains one of our contemporary lay theologians, "that brings men to Christ but contact with Christ that brings men to the consciousness of sin."[3] Animals also experience anxiety and guilt, but only man can respond to God in full self-consciousness.

To continue reminding men of their sinfulness may not be the message of Christ for this moment in history. Why always wait until the house is on fire? Is there no preventive? The church may serve as a hospital, but it is more than that. It is also a community of learners, learning to become human beings under God. While a consciousness of guilt is necessary, the Christian faith goes much beyond that.

Beyond Guilt

Forgiveness of sin must again become a part of God's pedagogy so that Christ truly becomes our Exemplar. God is not only judge; he is also our Father. "Christ stands at the center of all meaning because he shows us who God is and what he wants for us by himself being the decisive Exemplar of the whole learning process. . . . The purpose of creation is to learn to live the life of love. *Creation is for education.*"[4] And the purpose of God's incarnation in Christ is not only that we might be forgiven but that we might be enabled to follow him in a life of obedience and servanthood. In fact, even beyond that it is of the Spirit's guidance and gifts that we learn to accept ourselves as children of God's family and move about freely among fellows who are also on the way. This is the fullest freedom within responsible love available to us.

It may well be that one of the grandest rediscoveries of our day, especially among traditional churches, is the importance and finality of the Holy Spirit in our lives. But the moment we underscore this we are saturating our theology with educational perspectives. For the Spirit not only convicts us of sin—which in itself leads to futility—but also leads us into truth. When one has been led into the truth, hostility and hatred, divisiveness and destruction, are on the way out.

Love is not only a gift of the Spirit, it is the Spirit. Hence the best way to discover what the church is is to join in the fellowship of the Spirit. God does not insist on compulsory attendance in his school, for one can decide to be a drop-out. It is possible to discover to the fullest what Whitehead called "the romance in education," but one can also proceed to the ultimate in futility—the sin against the Holy Spirit.

In this connection we refer again to the utter futility of any attempt to teach without involvement. We are not here to study ancient history but to learn how to live. This happens primarily through participation. For religious instruction is not primarily a study of the Bible as literature or a history of the Judeo-Christian faith or Christian ethics or contemporary world mission. The fact that the Christian faith is not a body of knowledge but a way of life has always been a stumbling-block to intellectuals who like to analyze and theorize until these become ultimates. But often, while all these studies proceed, lowly samaritans are out leading wounded pilgrims to the inn.

Cult of Contemporaneity

Then what is the place of knowledge? Why study? How much knowledge must I possess in order to have faith? I cannot make faith's basic decisions in a vacuum.

The strength of the Christian faith lies not only in its present but also in its past and its future. Though often the church has been guilty of a false hero worship, as though only the past had any meaningful significance, man must be in vigorous conversation with his past. He may be unaware of this continuity or he can deliberately reject it.

Equally futile is the view of many who attempt to debunk

all history as useless—who in fact attempt to ignore the truth of the past in order not to be confronted by it. The present is judged by the past. For the Christian faith ultimate norms have come from the past, for Christ died once and for all. In times of anguish and frustration there is encouragement in the history of a fellowship which at its highest edge or its deepest commitment presents millions of martyrs and many lives lived in frustration with undaunted courage.

Encounter with Simplicity

The endless variations which have developed in the area of theology even the most brilliant theologian could not enumerate, much less decipher. This need not be documented.

It becomes an effort in futility to search out and rush after every change in the winds of doctrine. When the efforts of experts help then they are to be encouraged, and much that has appeared in the last few decades is of inestimable value in helping to make responsible decisions.

Yet in the end the greatest secret may well be an encounter with simplicity. In a day when even the reality of God is questioned and reexamined we dare not hide behind a multiplicity of arguments in order to avoid confrontation with the divine. We are prone to two errors: oversimplification and cynicism. Our task is to give honest though incomplete utterance to God's revelation and man's search for meaning.

It is not particularly difficult to conduct guided tours today through the wastelands of our contemporary problems with a running commentary on the global perils, the cultural malaise, or the personal dis-ease which confronts us all. Such a doleful assessment of the world is not biblical realism but a kind of sickness itself, with distortions scarcely less perilous than those it tries to correct. This is not speaking prophetically in the sense of Scripture, for such efforts lack what Paul Tillich called a "belief-ful realism," that "self-transcending historical realism which experiences the ultimate in and through a concrete historical situation." [5]

"Damn the day I was born. The night that said, 'A boy is begot'" (Job). [6]

Subsequently, Job comes to what other convictions?

For Further Discussion

1. "The fact is that man can fail to learn. He can refuse God's pedagogy. He can be dismissed from school for much or even the rest of his life. . . . So far our attempt has been to state a doctrine of the Christian understanding of the Trinity in educational terms: The Father as Educator; the Son as Exemplar; and the Holy Spirit as Tutor. In final meaning the primary terms remain, for they are eternally essential, but the pedagogical terms are the most meaningful for our created era." [7]

2. How many of the gifts of the Spirit are directed toward the growth of man?

3. What place does the fellowship of the Spirit have in our training? Have you ever sensed the pull of the Spirit among a group of Spirit-filled people?

4. What is the author trying to say? "Experience and judgment are always bound up with a *horizon* of openness towards reality, in which a thing comes to view and can be experienced and in which judgments become meaningful. A horizon of this kind contains a certain anterior knowledge of that which we learn. It is not a closed system, but includes also open questions and anticipation and is therefore open towards the new and the unknown." [8]

5. How are the following evidences of the demonic? Disruption, conflict, self-destruction, meaninglessness, lawlessness, narcotics addiction, despair.

6. In one of the greatest sermons of our day, entitled, "You Are Accepted," Paul Tillich describes the experiences in which "Grace strikes us." These include experiences of guilt, but also those when "we walk through the dark valley of a dark and meaningless and empty life." And he insists that no particular form or mode of the experience of acceptance can be prescribed. "Nothing is demanded of this experience, no religious, or moral, or intellectual presupposition. . . . *You are accepted*, accepted by that which is greater than you, and the name of which you do not know. Do not ask for the name now; perhaps you will find it later. Do not try to do anything now; perhaps you will later do much. Do not seek for anything; do not perform any-

thing; do not intend anything. Simply accept the fact that you are accepted." [9]

7. Is forgiveness the same as acceptance? Is this more than sheer cancellation of debts? How can it be a healing and creative function? Faith is the courage to be, and this must be an affirmation in which all anxieties can be overcome.

8. Is this a legitimate summary of minimal postulates of the Christian faith: The reality of God who revealed himself in a threefold manner, the divine creation of the universe, human sinfulness, divine incarnation in the person of Jesus, the Christ, his reconciliation of man to God, his founding of the Christian church and the continuing operation of his Spirit in the world, the primacy of love, man's responsibility to God, and an eventful end to human history culminating in the fulfillment of God's ultimate purpose for his creation. Does all this help me grow in my relationship to God and men, and in meeting the gut issues of our day?

9. What did the philosopher mean when he said: The greatest evil is to make abstract what is concrete?

10. Is there a bit of Sara's laugh in all of us?

11. If there were no evil or suffering, would we be driven back to ultimates, would we be satisfied with stock answers even more than now?

12. It has been stated that first-century man was concerned about death and immortality, sixteenth-century man about guilt and punishment, while twentieth-century man is disturbed by the threat of meaninglessness. What is our deepest or ultimate concern? Do we discuss this often—why or why not?

13. John Donne wrote, "No man is an island," Albert Camus maintained, "Every man is an island." Which one expresses your conviction?

14. A renowned scholar of the Old Testament suggests that the "woes" or maledictions of the prophets should be retranslated. They are not invectives but laments, more like dirges, saying: My heart cries out for you. Which translation approximates your image of God?

15. For many years some of us defended this progression: God → Church → World. Should it not be: God → World → Church? What is the difference?

16. "Reform will come, despite the spirit of our age! But not through one man—through the Church herself. Not, however, through the Church as a whole, but rather through a minority that lives in true communion with God. 'But those of the people who know their God shall be manly and shall achieve it' (Daniel 11:32).[10]

17. "If a government spends more resources on destroying lives than it does on creating the possibilities for fuller life . . . then such a government must be overthrown—even though it claims to be the paragon of democracy. Or, if a religious order spends more time and money on beautifying its physical plant . . . than it does on dealing with the problems which separate men from one another and from God, then that order must be overthrown—even though it calls itself Christian." [11]

18. "The fact that public worship in the local church, in the natural progression that it follows, is often a formal and at times a misunderstood pattern confirms and underlines the need for the church to share in examination and instruction in public worship, in Scripture, in Christian discipline, which the *sharing of small groups* best provides. . . . The small group, centered in biblical instruction and devotion and outreach, and in the shared intimate experience of Christ's presence, belongs in the center of the church's life." [12]

19. The question we probably hear from someone who missed church was, "What did he say?"—meaning, "What was the sermon about?" A new generation is more apt to ask, "What happened?" What did happen last Sunday?

20. The above paragraph may need to be balanced by this one: "The mission of the Christian is the way of love . . . we have spent too much time simply talking." [13]

21. Does God ever change? If not, how could he die? If yes, then what is God like? If God can do everything, then can he change?

Books for Suggested Reading

1. Letty Russell, *Christian Education in Mission.* Westminster, 1967.

2. G. W. Webber, *God's Colony in Man's World.* Abingdon, 1960.

3. J. Elliott Corbett, *The Prophets on Main Street.* John Knox, 1965.

4. Donald G. Bloesch, *The Christian Life and Salvation.* Eerdmans, 1967.

5. Jean-Paul Sartre, *Existentialism,* tr. B. Frechtman. Philosophical Library, 1947.

6. Bertrand Russell, *Why I am Not a Christian.* Simon and Schuster, 1957.

7. Martin Buber, *Two Types of Faith.* Macmillan, 1952.

8. Gustav Aulén, *The Faith of the Christian Church,* tr. Eric H. Wahlstrom. Fortress, 1960.

CHAPTER THIRTEEN

TELL ME ABOUT MY HOME

Ever since Charles Darwin initiated his theories of the evolution of man, men have been inordinately concerned about their beginnings. His studies certainly also gave impetus to countless inquiries about man himself. Once we ask how we got here, we cannot escape the next question: What is man? As valid and vital as these questions are, they ought always to be followed by a third: Where did we come from? Who are we? Where are we going? These are like the three legs of a tripod—remove one and the others are of little value.

Fortunately, there is a wholesome resurgence of interest today in the third question, which in many quarters had almost been ignored: Where are we going, and to what extent can man participate in determining his final destiny? All of us have a permanent encounter with death, and in the distance we still hear the faint echo of an atom bomb survivor: "I have seen the end of the world."

Three prefatory statements are in order. The first is that we ought to approach this subject with a great amount of trepidation. The moment we speak of life after death we are dealing with an area in which we have no experiential knowledge. No one can say, "I have been there, and it is like this. . . ." Possibly that is the reason why we have so much difficulty with the beginning and the end, creation and consummation.

One other assertion should also be underscored: Life has no meaning until death makes sense. For that reason most religions have something to offer in the future. The Indians have their Happy Hunting Ground and the Buddhists have their Nirvana. Even Marxism is filled with promises of a better future and a classless state. If death, which we cannot avoid, is a meaningless experience, then life is absurd. Death may be inevitable, unescapable, unrehearsable, unexplainable, and final—but is it the end?

Any discussion of this subject must keep in mind the fact that a theology of hope need not lead to quietism. To sing with feeling "Heaven is my home" may be a poor substitute for concerned social action. One can escape social upheavals and stark starvation by mouthing lovely phrases about a glorious future that awaits those who remain faithful, forgetting that if one is full of faith in Christ he will emulate his love for others. But neither should social sensitivity erase all concern for a final consummation. Our faith is nurtured by hope—the two dare not be divorced.

Theology of Hope

This subject, we must admit, is an extremely elusive one from the viewpoint of the Christian faith. Too easily and too often Christian theology has given the impression that a discussion of eschatology or the end or eternity or the consummation is like an appendix loosely attached to the main body of our beliefs, when in reality it permeates everything else. "The eschatological is not one element *of* Christianity, but it is the medium of Christian faith as such, the key in which everything in it is set, the glow that suffuses everything here in the dawn of an expected new day . . . the eschatological outlook is characteristic of all Christian proclamation, of every Christian existence and of the whole Church. There is therefore only one real problem in Christian theology, which its own object forces upon it and which it in turn forces on mankind and on human thought: the problem of the future." [1]

Because of all the nuances involved, every phrase becomes important when discussing our future. Great minds have occupied themselves in every age with this subject. Some believe that time, or history, is like a giant wheel going around and around. The future? It is simply the past over and over again. Nations rise and fall, individuals come and go. This view is a very depressing one, though probably quite popular. Others believe that "history is redemptive"—that is, day by day everything gets better and better. Occasionally there may be setbacks, but in the end progress is inevitable. This view appeals especially in our day of technological advances. Still others maintain that time corrodes, for everything is becoming worse, every generation is worse than the former one, and the times are out of joint more than ever.

The Christian Gospel asserts that time has a beginning and an end, and, above all, that it has a center in Jesus Christ. "He is our hope" (Colossians 1:27) may be the best and most succinct statement we can make about our future (cf. also Romans 8: 24-25). All of history receives meaning because of Christ's incarnation, death, and resurrection. The Old Testament looks forward to him, the New Testament remembers him, and we find our hope in him. Many images are used to elaborate upon this: the end of the age, the new Jerusalem coming down out of heaven from God, the consummation, the last judgment, the fulfillment, eternal life, salvation, Christ's second coming.

The assertion that "man is immortal," as though there were something within us that lives on, is an unfortunate one in this connection. We shall all die, but God will re-create us, resurrect us from death.

The question as to where we are between death and resurrection becomes largely academic and useless if our hope remains in Christ. There is no "where" in eternity, for "where" is a spatial term. The Bible states that the dead are asleep, but it also maintains that the redeemed sing praises around the throne of the Lamb. No on seems to have solved this mystery.

And it is not our major concern to solve it but simply to rejoice in God's love. For long after the atomic ovens have grown cold God's people will rejoice in the city which "has no need of sun or moon to shine upon it, for the glory of God is its light, and its lamp is the Lamb" (Revelation 21:23). The city was there long before we heard of it. The charts showing the way are old but no newer edition will be printed. Sometimes we can almost see the city, then again it is clouded with fog and smog. A long line of saints has preceded us on the way. Like myself, some have problems, but as pilgrims we help bear one another's burdens. We need not lose heart, for we already have the "down payment" that Paul had when he despaired of life (thoughts of suicide?) —namely, "his Spirit in our hearts" (2 Corinthians 1:22, 5:5; Ephesians 1:14).

Cosmic Redemption

Tell me about my home. And who will be there?

If the previous question of life after death was riddled with unsolved questions, then this one is even more difficult to answer.

While there are many variations, basically two theories are advanced.

One underscores all those biblical statements which limit heaven to the "believers." "He who believes and is baptized will be saved."

The other emphasis quotes primarily those statements of Scripture which seem to promise a cosmic redemption. "All men are to be saved and come to the knowledge of the truth." "There will be one fold and one shepherd." Not to be ignored is the sixfold repetition in Colossians 1 of the Christ who will be "all in all."

Until we have more information than is now available, we shall have to let this paradox stand unsolved. In the meantime we cry, "Come, Creator Spirit." There is only one other cry of the people of God that is comparable to this in poignancy and power and that is "Maranatha—Lord, come." Ultimately these two are one cry.

Social Imperatives

During the best days of her existence the church maintained a wholesome balance between the tension and the comfort that accompany any discussion of the future.

Precisely because we have a theology of hope, we also face social imperatives. If a better future awaits us, then why not already improve the present? Because of our conviction that history has a goal we can question every institution, including the church, out of openness for the future. "The hope of the gospel has a polemic and liberating relation not only to the religions and ideologies of men, but still more to the factual, practical life of men and to the relationships in which this life is lived. . . . In practical opposition to things as they are, and in creative reshaping of them, Christian hope calls them in question and thus serves the things that are to come." [2]

It is a bit surprising that our generation, which is experiencing so many new discoveries in almost every field of human endeavor, should expect so little that is new from the church. But there is a real tension between the old and the new already in the basic writings of the Christian faith, with the promise that the new will prevail. For if there is nothing new, then there is no hope.

One of the last statements of our Lord was the promise, "Behold I make all things new." There is to be a new heaven, a new earth, a new Jerusalem, new wine, a new song, a new man, a new commandment, a new tongue, a new testament.

It may be one of the most tragic happenings of our age that the hope of something new has moved out of the church. Christianity became a religion; it cultivated tradition, and Christians felt that they were recipients of an old message rather than pioneers and trailblazers of the future. Hope always rests on the past—"May my right arm wither if I forget you, Jerusalem"—but it does not stay there. "Pay no heed to former things." Read also 2 Corinthians 5.

Renewal always proclaims judgment on the old. Some things in our church will have to be destroyed and die before the new grain can grow. The first time the word Gospel appears in the Bible is after a lot of suffering and anguish (cf. Isaiah). And Mary's Magnificat promised that out of bad and evil good would come, because the same God would continue to serve his people.

If the Christian's approach to the future is not one of imminent Utopia, neither is it one of despair. We need to tell each other about the home that awaits us, or as another expressed it long ago, "comfort one another with these words," a statement that was made in connection with death and judgment (1 Thessalonians 4:18). There will be a day when demonic powers will be bound, otherwise there would be dualism, like two straight lines going on endlessly. "I am the Alpha and the Omega, the first and the last, the beginning and the end" (Revelation 22:13), a significant assertion of our Lord, is already now in the process of fulfillment.

A Theology of the Cross

Occasionally it is annoying not to find clear answers to ultimate questions. Certainly in these pages very few positive assertions have been posited, even in the area of faith's basic concerns.

Is there then so little certainty? Yes, especially for people who live by faith. Certitude was never a favorite word of saints. One of them, Martin Luther, summarized this emphasis in what is sometimes termed a "theology of the cross."

In the emerging holy catholic church Rome could teach us how to practice reflection and worship; Methodists should remind us of our responsibility in social concerns; Presbyterians can contribute a fine sensitivity in political acumen; while some of the Pentecostals may remind us of the joy of sacrificial giving. This grand symphony will also be enriched if Luther's emphasis on a theology of the cross is retained. Three thrusts may summarize the essential nature of this emphasis.

Phoniness

A theology of the cross attempts to avoid as much phoniness as possible. In the heat of disputation Luther wrote,

"19. The one who beholds what is invisible of God, through the perception of what is made (cf. Romans 1:20) is not rightly called a theologian.

"20. But rather the one who perceives what is visible of God, God's 'backside' (Exodus 33:23), by beholding the sufferings and the cross.

"21. The 'theologian of glory' calls the bad good and the good bad. The 'theologian of the cross' says what a thing is.

"22. That wisdom which beholds the invisible things of God as perceived from works—puffs up, blinds, and hardens man altogether.

"23. The law also brings about the wrath of God—it kills, reviles, makes guilty, judges, condemns all that is not in Christ.

"24. Nevertheless, this wisdom is not bad nor is the law to be fled. But without a theology of the cross, man misuses the best things in the worst way." [3]

God's Hiddenness

Basic to a theology of the cross is also the concept of God's hiddenness *(deus absconditus)*. Luther loved to quote Isaiah 45:15, "Truly thou art a God who hidest thyself, O God of Israel, the Savior," or Proverbs, "It is the glory of God to conceal." At another time he shouts, "God in diapers, God at the breast of Mary, God at a carpenter's bench? God on a cross? Who would think to look for him there?" Precisely. We do not find him; he comes to us, and he comes in a way that we do not expect of a Lord.

Since this issue is extremely acute in our day Paul Tillich went a step farther and asserted, "Why is God absent? Because of our resistance, our indifference? The final answer is: it is the work of the Spirit that removes God from our sight, not only for some men, but sometimes for many in a particular period. We live in an era in which the God we know is the absent God . . . the Spirit can hide itself and that means it can hide God." [4] The Spirit can hide God, but does he?

Anfechtung

Of value to us is also the stress on *Anfechtung*—trial, temptation, affliction, anguish, assaults. According to a theology of the cross there is no faith without *Anfechtung*.

"Show us the Father," said Philip, asking for a theology of glory. "He who has seen me has seen the Father," replied Jesus with a theology of the cross, an answer which is not grasped by reason but by faith. For some the Christian life seems to begin with knowledge (cf. Karl Barth, *Kirchliche Dogmatik*, 11/1, p. 12); for others it is trust. And the answer to *Anfechtung* is not knowledge but trust, since "In all *Anfechtung*," says Luther, "we are dealing directly with God."

Often dramatists and poets and artists have sensed this with real depth. One of them wrote a simple play depicting the journey of Joseph and Mary and the Child to Egypt. After they had gone far enough to feel secure, the three are resting around a campfire in the evening's cool shadows. Joseph and Mary reminisce. They rehearse once more the fabulous events of Christmas Eve, and with each retelling the events become more glorious. In the midst of their reverie their donkey turns his head—if a donkey could speak in the Old Testament, there should be one also in the New! —and speaks his one line. He says slowly and deliberately to Mary and Joseph, "And to think that the fate of the whole world rests on my shoulders."

For Further Discussion

1. What words, phrases, expressions in this chapter are without meaning for you? Who can help?

2. With which of the following do you associate the element of newness? Science, church, Marxism, education? Do any of these remind you of a prefabricated house?

3. Do you find any "tremors of eschatology" in the following: the day of the Lord, the exile and captivity, the exodus, revolt and wars of independence, new age, a new heaven and a new earth, Revelation 21, 1 Corinthians 15? Could each member of the group develop one of these emphases?

4. How does a hidden God differ from no God at all?

5. What do Roman Catholics mean when they speak of beatific vision?

6. Can you hope for the future without remembering the past? Do men still ask: Is there any hope? A Christianity without hope has been compared to a man who holds an electric cord in his hand but fails to plug it in.

7. What do we need more: an answer to sin or an answer to death?

8. Why do Marxists have funerals? What is Christian about our funerals? What is more important than to argue about cremation?

9. Would you agree with the Broadway actor who cried out in a play, "There's a tug of war within me, and both sides are losing"? If Jesus can agonize about being forsaken by God, cannot the same thing happen to us?

10. "In the Christian life faith has the priority, but hope the primacy. Without faith's knowledge of Christ, hope becomes a Utopia and remains hanging in the air. But without hope, faith

falls to pieces, becomes a fainthearted and ultimately a dead faith. It is through faith that man finds the path of true life, but it is only hope that keeps him on that path." [5]

11. "So faith, hope, love abide, these three; but the greatest of these is love" (1 Corinthians 13:13).

12. We have teachers of church history; why do we not have teachers of the church's future? What does the expression "Lord of history" say to you?

13. Do you think of creation as something that happened in the past or as a continuing act of God? What is the difference? Is this only an academic distinction?

14. Is this a good interpretation of Hebrews 11:1? "To us is given the promise of eternal life—but to us, the dead. A blessed resurrection is proclaimed to us—meantime we are surrounded by decay. We are called righteous—and yet sin lives in us. We hear of ineffable blessedness—but meantime we are here oppressed by infinite misery. We are promised abundance of all good things— yet we are rich only in hunger and thirst. What would become of us if we did not take our stand on hope, and if our heart did not hasten beyond this world through the midst of the darkness upon the path illumined by the Word and Spirit of God! . . . Hope is nothing else than the expectation of those things which faith has believed to have been truly promised by God . . . hope nourishes and sustains faith." [6]

15. "We do not hope for ourselves alone, nor for those who share our hope. We also hope for those who had and now have not hope, for those whose hopes for this life remain unfulfilled, for those who are disappointed and indifferent, for those who despair of life and even for those who have hurt or destroyed life. Certainly if we hoped only for ourselves and not also for our world, it would be a poor and selfish hope." [7]

16. Which of the following are open or closed questions:

    a. Christ will come again.

    b. The church must speak out on social issues.

    c. The dead are still conscious.

d. The end of the world is very near, it is five minutes to twelve.

e. Heaven is not a place but a state of being.

f. If God is love, then all will be saved.

g. Christ hides himself in the stable of human history.

h. Americans are more concerned about space than about time.

i. The fullness of time is the same as the end of the world.

17. What different emphases do the following underscore concerning the consummation—Jesus, Paul, John, James? Is there a single page in the New Testament which does not in some way have eschatological overtones? Why does the Book of Revelation have a peculiar fascination? What is meant by apocalypse?

18. What is Karl Barth trying to say with this statement: "A Christianity which is not altogether and utterly eschatological has altogether and utterly nothing to do with Jesus Christ"?

19. This is worth pondering: "I think what we need now is to pull forward the eschatological profundity of the Church's tradition. Eschatology is simply that discipline of theology which deals with the limit of all things, temporal, historical, and human, and which postulates the persistence of the divine life behind, above, and beyond these limitations. This is that resource, that bottom drawer in the church's massive filing cabinet, which may have to be unpacked for this generation." [8]

20. "Missions perform their service today only when they infect men with hope." [9]

21. Kierkegaard once remarked that time tables are not very interesting unless you are going somewhere.

22. "If I should live a little while longer," wrote a mature Luther in 1530, "I would like to write a book about *Anfechtung*. Without it no man can rightly understand the Holy Scriptures or know what the fear and love of God is all about. In fact, without *Anfechtung* one does not really know what the spiritual life is." [10]

23. Since Luther asserted "that a theologian is born by living,

nay, dying and being damned, not by thinking, reading and speculating," the following summary may well be true: "Research in Luther which has been associated with neo-Reformation theology . . . has the merit of pointing to the theologia crucis as normative for Luther's understanding of theology. It has established that this was not only an important section of his thought, but the pivot around which everything gravitates." [11]

24. Do you know of a better approach? " . . . when I am with someone who has suffered a bereavement I often decide to adopt a 'penultimate' attitude, remaining silent as a sign that I share in the bereaved man's helplessness in the face of such a grievous event, and not speaking the biblical words of comfort which are, in fact, known to me and available to me. . . . Is it because of some mistrust of the ultimate word? Or is there some good positive reason for such an attitude, namely, that my knowledge of the word, my having it at my fingertips, in other words, my being, so to speak, spiritually master of the situation, bears only the appearance of the ultimate, but is in reality itself something entirely penultimate? Does one not in some cases, by remaining deliberately in the penultimate, perhaps point all the more genuinely to the ultimate, which God will speak in His own time. . . ." [12]

25. Immanuel Kant maintained that we have three major questions:

    a. What can I know?

    b. What ought I to do?

    c. What may I hope? In trying to answer these has the Christian church kept a wholesome balance?

26. Which of the old hymns speaks meaningfully of our Christian hope? Is there a recent song which says it equally well? Why not sing them both?

27. There's a touch of homesickness in the Christian's heart whenever he says, "I look for the resurrection of the dead, and the life of the world to come."

28. When Buddha was asked by his students whether the world was finite or not, or whether the universe is eternal, he answered,

"I do not know and it is of no concern to me because whatever the answer is it does not contribute to the one problem which is of concern: how to reduce human suffering." (Cf. John 13:35.)

29. "This heavenly city . . . while it sojourns on earth, calls citizens out of all nations, and gathers together a society of pilgrims of all languages, not scrupling about diversities . . . but recognizing that, however various these are, they all tend to one and the same end of earthly peace . . . and that seventh age will be our sabbath, a day that knows no evening, but is followed by the day of the Lord, an everlasting eighth day, hallowed by the resurrection of Christ, prefiguring the eternal rest not only of the spirit, but of the body as well. Then we shall have holiday and we shall see, we shall see and we shall love, we shall love and we shall praise. Behold, this is how it shall be at the end without end. For what else is our end, but to come to that kingdom which has no end?" [13]

Books for Suggested Reading

1. William Stringfellow, *Free in Obedience*. Seabury, 1967.

2. Dietrich Ritschl, *Memory and Hope*. Macmillan, 1967.

3. John Dillenberger, *God Hidden and Revealed*. Muhlenberg (Fortress), 1953.

4. John Strietelmeyer, *Off-Key Praises*. Concordia, 1967.

5. Charles Y. Glock, Benjamin B. Ringer, Earl R. Babbie, *To Comfort and to Challenge*. University of California Press, 1967.

6. Paul Minear, *Christian Hope and the Second Coming*. Westminster, 1954.

7. Hans J. Margull, *Hope in Action*. Muhlenberg (Fortress), 1962.

8. Jaroslav Pelikan, *The Shape of Death*. Abingdon, 1961.

ACKNOWLEDGMENTS

for quotations used by permission

Chapter I

Condemned to Meaning

1. Nels F. S. Ferré, *Searchlights on Contemporary Theology* (Harper, 1961), p. 43.
2. *A New Catechism*, tr. Kevin Smyth (Copyright 1967 Herder and Herder, 232 Madison Ave., New York, N.Y. 10016), p. V.
3. *The Christian Century*, May 25, 1966, p. 674. Copyright 1966 Christian Century Foundation.
4. Paul Tillich, "Communicating the Gospel," *Union Seminary Quarterly*, June 1952, pp. 3 and 4.
5. Amos N. Wilder, *Early Christian Rhetoric. The Language of the Gospel* (Harper, 1966).
6. C. H. Dodd, *The Bible Today* (Cambridge University, 1952), p. 104.

Chapter II

Viable Alternatives

1. Marshall McLuhan, *Understanding Media* (Copyright 1965 McGraw Hill), pp. IX, 26.
2. Erich Fromm, "The Limitations and Dangers of Psychology," in *Religion and Culture*, ed. Walter Leibrecht (Harper, 1959), p. 36.
3. *Systematic Theology* (University of Chicago, 1951-63, II), p. 13.
4. Hugh Montefiore, "Renewal of the Church," in *Encounter*, Spring 1966, p. 103
5. W. A. Visser't Hooft, *The Christian Century*, July 5, 1967, p. 864. Copyright 1967 Christian Century Foundation.
6. Warren Quanbeck in *The Lutheran*, March 13, 1968, p. 30.
7. Steven Kelnan, "Parent and Child," in *The New York Times Magazine*, October 22, 1967, p. 146. Copyright 1967 New York Times Company.
8. David Earle Anderson, in *The Lutheran Standard*, September 19, 1967, pp. 2 and 5.
9. Søren Kierkegaard, *Christian Discourses*, tr. Walter Lowrie (Oxford University, 1939), p. 248.
10. John A. T. Robinson, *The New Reformation?* (Copyright 1965 SCM Press, Ltd.), p. 34. Published in the U.S.A. by The Westminster Press, 1965.

Chapter III
Who Has the Lantern?

1. Walter Eichrodt, *Man in the Old Testament,* tr. K. and R. Gregor Smith (Regnery, 1952), p. 9.
2. Joseph R. Barndt, *Why Black Power* (Friendship, 1968), pp. 24 and 25.
3. Teenager, quoted in *Risk,* Vol. III, No. 3, p. 16.
4. Paul Lehmann, *Ethics in a Christian Context* (SCM, 1963), p. 26.
5. Roger Garaudy, *From Anathema to Dialogue,* tr. Luke O'Neill (Copyright 1966 Herder and Herder, 232 Madison Ave., New York, N.Y. 10016), p. 109.
6. Johannes C. Hoeckendijk, in *Lutheran World,* 1967, Vol. I, p. 6.
7. Teilhard de Chardin. (Exact source not known.)

Chapter IV
God

1. Abraham Heschel, *God in Search of Man* (Farrar, Straus, and Cudahy, Inc., 1955), p. 187.
2. Wolfhart Pannenberg, "The Question of God," in *Interpretation,* July 1967, p. 309.
3. Leslie Dewart, *The Future of Belief* (Copyright 1967 Herder and Herder, 232 Madison Ave., New York, N.Y. 10016), pp. 167, 214.
4. Lutheran World Federation Assembly, Helsinki, 1963.
5. Eric Hoffer, *The True Believer* (Harper, 1951), p. 114.
6. Paul Tillich, *Theology of Culture* (Oxford University, 1959).
7. Otto Rank in *The Death and Rebirth of Psychology* by Ira Progoff (Julian, 1956), p. 251.
8. Reinhold Niebuhr, in *Reinhold Niebuhr, His Religious, Social and Political Thought,* C. W. Kegley and R. W. Bretall, eds., *The Library of Living Theology,* Vol. III, 1956, p. 446.
9. Cyril C. Richardson, *The Doctrine of the Trinity* (Abingdon, 1958).
10. Abraham Heschel, *op. cit.,* p. 116 and p. 187.
11. *The Lutheran World,* 1967, Vol. I, p. 7.
12. Leslie Dewart, *op. cit.,* p. 171.

Chapter V
Planned History

1. Cf. A. T. van Leeuwen, *Christianity in World History,* tr. H. H. Hoskins (Scribners, 1964).

2. Paul Tillich, *Theology of Culture* (Oxford University, 1959), p. 213.

3. Gustaf Wingren, *Gospel and Church*, tr. Ross Mackenzie (Fortress, 1964), pp. 99, 106, 166.

Chapter VI
Bearded Tradition

1. Karl Barth, *The Doctrine of the Word of God*, 2nd Ed. (Scribner 1949).

2. Cf. 23rd Psalm from Carl F. Burke, *God Is for Real, Man* (Association Press, 1966), or Malcolm Boyd's prayers.

3. *A New Catechism, op. cit.*, p. VIII.

4. H. W. Bartsch, ed., *Kerygma and Myth* (Harper, 1961), p. 4.

5. Karl Barth, *Epistle to the Romans*, tr. Sir Edwyn Haskyns (Oxford University, 1933), p. 425.

6. Gerhard von Rad, *Studies in Deuteronomy*, tr. David Stalker (SCM, 1953), p. 70. Published in U.S.A. by Allenson.

7. Otto Rank, in Ira Progoff, *The Death and Rebirth of Psychology* (Julian, 1956), p. 251.

8. Dietrich Bonhoeffer, *Letters and Papers from Prison*, ed. Eberhard Bethge (SCM, 1967), p. 172.

9. Ian Ramsey, *Religious Language* (Macmillan, 1957), p. 12.

10. Richard Kroner, *The Religious Function of Imagination* (Yale University, 1941), p. 46.

11. Helmut Thielicke, *The Trouble with the Church* (Harper, 1965), p. 39.

Chapter VII
Has the Church Betrayed Christ?

1. *What in the World* (National Council of Churches, 1965), p. 12.

2. Daniel Jenkins, *Beyond Religion* (Westminster. Copyright © 1962 Daniel Jenkins), p. 113.

3. Eugene Carson Blake, *The Church in the Next Decade* (Macmillan, 1966), pp. 17 and 24.

4. European Lutheran-Reformed Conversation 1967, *Risk*, Vol. III, No. 3, p. 38.

5. Harvey G. Cox, "The 'New Breed' in American Churches: Sources of Social Activism in American Religion," in *Daedalus*, Journal of the American Academy of Arts and Sciences, Boston (Winter 1967, "Religion in America"), p. 136.

6. George A. Lindbeck, "Reformed Conversation—European Lutheran," in *Risk*, Vol. III, No. 3, 1967, p. 38.

7. Billy Graham, quoted in *The Christian Century*, September 27, 1967, p. 1213. Copyright 1967 Christian Century Foundation.

8. F. W. Dillistone, *The Structure of the Divine Society* (Westminster. Copyright © 1951 W. L. Jenkins).

9. Martin Luther, *Sämtliche Schriften* (J. G. Walch), Band IX, 1386.

10. John Calvin, *Institutes of the Christian Religion*, Preface, 1559 ed. C R, XXX.

11. *Dialog*, Winter, 1965, p. 4.

12. Canon C. Southcott, *The Christian Century*, December 5, 1962, p. 1486. Copyright 1962 Christian Century Foundation.

13. T. George Harris, "The Battle of the Bible," in *Look*, July 27, 1965, p. 4.

14. John H. Wagner Jr., from an address on: "Renewal of Mission in the Lutheran Church in Brooklyn."

15. Quoted from an ecumenical document by Louise Stoltenberg in her article "What's Wrong with 'Church Renewal'?" appearing in *Christianity Today*, April 23, 1965, p. 4.

16. *Christianity and Crisis*, March 22, 1965, p. 56.

17. Harvey Cox, *The Secular City* (Macmillan, 1965), p. 105.

18. Archie Hargraves, *Social Action*, February 1964, p. 17.

19. *Religion in Life*, Spring 1965, p. 209.

20. *The Christian Century*, April 7, 1965, p. 446.

21. Robert W. Spike, *To Be a Man* (Association Press).

22. Daniel T. Niles, in a pamphlet published by World Mission Prayer League.

Chapter VIII

Dialogue Without Prejudice

1. Roger Garaudy, *From Anathema to Dialogue*, tr. Luke O'Neill (Copyright 1966 Herder and Herder, 232 Madison Ave., New York, N.Y. 10016), pp. 19-20 and 23.

2. *Ibid.*, p. 31.

3. Reuel Howe, *The Miracle of Dialogue* (Copyright © 1962 Seabury Press), p. 70.

4. Hans Ruedi Weber, *Salty Christians* (Copyright © 1963 Seabury Press), p. 16.

5. *The Church for Others* (World Council of Churches, 1967), p. 91.
6. William Pauck, in *Religion and Culture*, ed. Walter Leibrecht (Harper, 1959), p. 282.
7. John T. McNeill, *Unitive Protestantism* (John Knox, 1964), p. 14.
8. The Westminster Confession of Faith, in Philip Schaff, ed., *The Creeds of Christendom* (Harper, 1877), Vol. III, p.658.
9. Calvin, *op. cit.*, C R, XXX, 759.
10. *The National Observer*, March 11, 1968, p. 11.
11. *A New Catechism, op. cit.*, p. 27.
12. Jaroslav Pelikan, in *Una Sancta*, Vol. 23, No. 3, p. 6.
13. *A New Catechism, op. cit.*, p. 226.
14. Wolfhart Pannenberg, in *Una Sancta*, Vol. 24, No. 4, p. 11.
15. *Initiative in History: A Christian-Marxist Exchange*, an occasional paper published by the Church Society for College Work, 2 Brewer Street, Cambridge, Mass., 1967: Inho page 2, col. B; Garaudy page 8, col. B; Blanchebbe page 21, col. B.
16. Harvey Cox in *Dialog*, Winter 1968, p. 24.
17. Eugene Carson Blake, in *The Christian Century*, July 20, 1966, p. 906. Copyright 1966 Christian Century Foundation.

Chapter IX

Inside the Cup

1. Stephen C. Rose, "Protestantism: Dead or Alive?" in *Risk*, 1966, IV (World Council of Churches and World Council of Religious Education, Geneva, Switzerland), p. 66.
2. John W. Gardner, *Self-Renewal* (Harper, 1963), p. 5.
3. *Chicago Tribune*, January 1, 1967, p. 7.
4. John W. Gardner, *Self-Renewal* (Harper, 1963), p. 37.
5. *The Faith of the Christian Church*, tr. Eric H. Wahlstrom (Muhlenberg [Fortress], 1960), pp. 336-337.
6. C. F. D. Moule, Adam and Charles Black, *The Birth of the New Testament* (London: A. & C. Black; New York: Marper 1962), p. 130.
7. Martin Luther, *The Bondage of the Will*, tr. J. I. Packer and O. R. Johnston (Revell 1957), p. 319.
8. Daniel Day Williams, "The New Theological Situation," in *Theology Today*, January, 1968, p. 444. Johnston (London, 1957), p. 319.
9. A. T. van Leeuwen, *Christianity in World History*, tr. H. H. Haskins (Scribners, 1964).

10. Colin Williams, *Where in the World* (National Council of Churches, U.S.A., 1963), p. 33.

11. Richard John Neuhaus, in *Una Sancta*, Vol. 23, No. 2, p. 81.

12. Paul Tillich, *Systematic Theology*, III (University of Chicago), p. 166.

13. Richard Luecke, *New Meanings for New Beings* (Fortress, 1964), p. 97.

14. Gibson Winter, *The New Creation as Metropolis* (Macmillan, 1963).

Chapter X

Renewal of Man

1. Paul Tillich, *Systematic Theology*, III (University of Chicago), p. 210.

2. World Council of Churches, Second Assembly, Evanston, Ill., 1954.

3. Hans Ruedi Weber, *Salty Christians* (Copyright © 1963 Seabury Press), p. 28.

4. Karl Rahner, *Theology for Renewal* (Sheed and Ward, 1964).

5. Paul Tillich, *Systematic Theology*, Vol. III (University of Chicago, 1963), p. 194.

6. Otto Weber, in *Lutheran World*, October 1964, p. 435.

7. George W. Webber, in *Theological Education*, Vol. I, No. 1, p. 26.

8. Granger E. Westberg, in *Lutheran Quarterly*, May 1967, p. 116.

9. Gerald H. Slusser, *The Local Church in Transition* (Westminster. Copyright © 1964 J. L. Jenkins), p. 178.

10. Paul M. Van Buren, *The Secular Meaning of the Gospel* (Macmillan, 1963), p. 204.

11. *Time* Magazine, Dec. 25, 1964, p. 48.

12. Johannes C. Hoekendijk, *The Church Inside Out*, tr. Isaac C. Rottenberg (Westminster. Copyright © 1966 J. L. Jenkins), p. 80.

13. H. Richard Niebuhr, *Purpose of the Church and Its Ministry* (Harper, 1956), p. 78.

14. T. W. Manson, *Ministry and Priesthood* (John Knox, 1959), p. 21.

15. *Renewal*, December 1965, p. 2.

16. Wolfenden Report.

17. Harvey Cox, in *Motive*, November 1965, pp. 8 and 9.

18. Herbert Butterfield, *The Origin of Modern Science* (Macmillan, 1958), pp. VII and VIII.

Chapter XI

Capitulation or Revolution?

1. *The Christian Scholar* (National Council of Churches), Winter, 1965, p. 297.
2. Paul M. Van Buren, in *The Christian Century*, April 7, 1965, p. 430. Copyright 1965 Christian Century Foundation.
3. J. A. T. Robinson. (Exact source unknown.)
4. Dietrich Bonhoeffer, *Ethics* (Macmillan, 1955), p. 131.
5. ————, *Toward a Quaker View of Sex* (Friends Book Store, Philadelphia), p. 45.
6. *Ibid.,* p. 45.
7. *Laity Bulletin* (World Council of Churches, July 1967), p. 23.
8. Tom F. Driver, "Taking Sex Seriously," in *Christianity and Crisis,* October 14, 1963, p. 176.
9. Carl C. Zimmerman and Lucius F. Cervantes, *Marriage and the Family* (Regnery, 1956), p. 118.
10. Oliver Chadwick, tr., *Of the Rule of St. Benedict* (Westminster, 1958), Chapter 7.
11. James Sellers, *Theological Ethics* (Macmillan, 1966), Preface.
12. Michael Novak, in *Commonweal,* July 1967, p. 441.
13. Joseph Sittler, Address on "The Role of Spirit in Creating the Future Environment."
14. *Renewal,* December 1965, p. 10.
15. Confession of 1967.
16. Paul Lehmann, *Ethics in a Christian Context* (Harper, 1963), pp. 120, 124, 135.
17. Erich Fromm, *Psychoanalysis and Religion* (Yale University, 1950), p. 63.

Chapter XII

Anatomy of Futility

1. Erich Fromm, "Individual and Social Origins of Neurosis," in *American Sociological Review,* IX, 1944, p. 384.
2. Dietrich Bonhoeffer, *Letters and Papers from Prison* (SCM, 1953).
3. Hendrik Kraemer. (Exact source unknown.)
4. Nels Ferré, *A Theology for Christian Education* (Copyright © 1967 Westminster Press), p. 138.
5. Paul Tillich, in *The Protestant Era* (University of Chicago 1948),

6. *The Anchor Bible,* tr. Marvin H. Pope (Doubleday, 1965), p. 26.
7. Nels Ferré, *op. cit.,* pp. 145, 150.
8. Jürgen Moltmann, *The Theology of Hope,* tr. James W. Leitch (Harper, 1967), pp. 190 and 191.
9. Paul Tillich, *The Shaking of the Foundations* (Scribner, 1948), p. 162.
10. Otto Dibelius, in *The National Lutheran,* October 1966, p. 3.
11. *Skandalon,* Winter 1967, p. 3.
12. Frederick M. Meek, "Some Answers to Critics," in *Religion in Life,* Spring 1965, p. 212.
13. Paul M. Van Buren, *The Secular Meaning of the Gospel* (Macmillan, 1963), p. 184.

Chapter XIII

Tell Me About My Home

1. Jürgen Moltmann, *The Theology of Hope,* tr. James W. Leitch (Harper, 1967), p. 16.
2. *Ibid.,* p. 330.
3. Heidelberg Disputation Theses of 1518, in John Dillenberger, *Martin Luther, Selections from His Writings* (Doubleday, 1961), p. 502.
4. *Union Seminary Quarterly,* January, 1962.
5. Jürgen Moltmann, *op. cit.,* p. 20.
6. John Calvin, *Institutes of the Christian Religion,* ed. John T. McNeill, tr. Ford Lewis Battles (Westminster, 1960), p. 590.
7. Paul Tillich, in *The Right to Hope* (Source not known).
8. Joseph Sittler, "Freedom and Responsibility" in *Proceedings of the Institute on Problems That Unite Us* (Sisters of Charity, BVM, Mt. Carmel, Dubuque, Iowa, 1966).
9. J. C. Hoekendijk. (Exact source unknown.)
10. *Table Talk* 4777 (Weimar Edition 1916, Vol. 4, p. 491).
11. John Dillenberger, *God Hidden and Revealed* (Muhlenberg [Fortress], 1935), p. 146.
12. Dietrich Bonhoeffer, *Ethics* (Macmillan, 1955), pp. 84, 85.
13. Augustine, *The City of God,* XIX, 7, and XXII, 30 (adapted from the Latin).

Index of Authors

Alinsky, S., 63, 67
Anderson, D. E., 13
Aptheker, H., 81
Augustinus, A., 108, 114, 137
Aulen, G., 125

Bach, J. S., 23
Bailey, S., 117
Bainton, R., 67
Barndt, J. R., 21
Barth, K., 46, 53, 132, 135
Bartsch, H. W., 43, 52
Bennett, J. C., 117
Berger, P., 76
Bernard de Clairvaux, 62
Berton, P., 81
Blake, E. C., 61, 67, 81
Bloch, E., 80
Bloesch, D. G., 125
Bonhoeffer, D., 32, 54, 62, 91, 96, 103, 106, 109, 114, 118, 119, 136
Bornkamm, G., 43
Bowden, J., 29
Brunner, E., 117
Bryan, W. J., 19
Buber, M., 30, 32, 34, 74, 76, 81, 125
Bultmann, R., 29
Bunyan, 91, 114
Burke, C. F., 56
Burtness, J. H., 117
Butterfield, H., 102

Calvin, J., 59, 60, 64, 78, 82, 108, 109, 111, 116, 117, 134
Camus, A., 9, 13, 26, 123
Chadwick, O., 113
Chagall, M., 74
Chardin, T. de, 23, 96
Coffin, S., 114
Constantine the Great, 59, 62, 101
Corbett, J. E., 125
Cox, H. G., 63, 64, 81, 102, 103

Darrow, C., 19
Darwin, C., 126
Davies, J. G., 94
Dewart, L., 29, 33, 34
Dibelius, O., 124
Dillenberger, J., 136, 138
Dillistone, F. W., 63
Dodd, C. H., 6
Dolan, R. R., 67
Doniger, S., 117
Donne, J., 123
Driver, T. F., 111
Dulles, A., 66

Edwards, D., 99
Eichrodt, W., 16, 24
Ellington, D., 31

Ferré, N. F. S., 4, 103, 122
Fey, H. E., 81
Fletcher, J., 117
Forell, G. W., 56
Frankl, V. E., 15
Fromm, E., 11, 24, 117, 118
Furlong, M., 94

Garaudy, R., 22, 75, 80
Gardner, J. W., 83, 89, 94
Gibbs, M., 15
Gilkey, L., 32, 94
Glock, C. Y., 138
Graham, W., 63
Greene, G., 31
Greenwood, E., 103
Griffin, J. H., 15

Hamilton, W., 114
Hargraves, A., 64
Harris, T. G., 64
Hazelton, R., 7, 24, 34, 54
Heschel, A., 26, 32
Hoeckendijk, J. C., 23, 100, 117, 135
Hoedendijk, H., vii

147

Hoffer, E., 29
Hoffman, R., 66
Hooft, W. A. V., 13
Hoskins, H. H., 81
Howe, R., 76, 81

Ignatius, Bishop of Antioch, 13

Jansen, J., 94
Jefferson, 114
Jenkins, D., 7, 61
John, Pope, 82, 83
Judy, M. T., 81

Kaesemann, E., 62
Kant, I., 136
Kelnan, S., 13
Kierkegaard, S., 13, 14, 32, 135
King, C., 24
King, M. L., 114
Knutson, K. S., 24
Kraemer, H., 119
Kroner, R., 55

Leeuwen, A. T., 37, 81, 91
Lehmann, P., 22, 116, 117
Lenski, G., 103
Lilje, H., 109
Lindbeck, G. A., 63
Luecke, R., 92
Luther, M., 6, 12, 24, 32, 42, 52, 59, 60, 64, 70, 76, 82, 83, 90, 100, 109, 111, 116, 117, 131, 132, 135, 136

MacLeod, G., 67
McLuhan, M., 8
McNeill, J. T., 77
Manson, T. W., 101
Margull, H. J., 138
Marshall, R., 34
Marty, M., 15, 67, 76
Marx, K., 23, 75, 119
Meek, F. M., 124
Michalson, C., 56
Minear, P., 67, 138
Moltmann, J., 122, 127, 134
Montefiore, H., 12
Morton, T. R., 15
Mott, J., 76

Moule, C. F. D., 89
Murray, M. H., 103

Neill, W., 56
Nelson, C. E., 24
Neuhaus, R. J., 92, 114
Niebuhr, H. R., 100
Niebuhr, R., 30, 117
Niemoeller, M., 109, 114
Niles, D. T., 66
Northcott, C., 5
Novak, M., 114, 115

Otto, R., 94

Pannenberg, W., 26, 80
Pauck, William, 77, 81
Payne, P., 67
Pelikan, J., 78, 138
Porteous, A. C., 43

Quanbeck, W., 13

Rad, G., 53
Rahner, K., 34, 98
Raines, R., 76, 103
Ramsey, I., 54
Ramsey, P., 117
Rank, O., 30, 54
Richardson, C. C., 31, 34
Ritschl, D., 138
Robinson, J. A. T., 14, 15, 106, 117
Rose, S. C., 67, 82
Rougemont, D., 54
Routley, E., 24
Ruether, R. R., 7
Russell, B., 55, 125
Russell, L., 125

Sartre, J-P., 15, 125
Schmithals, W., 29
Sittler, J., 103, 115, 135
Skibbe, E. M., 94
Slusser, G. H., 99
Smart, J. D., 7, 56, 103
Smith, H., 7
Southcott, C. C., 64
Spike, R. W., 66
Stendahl, K., 32
Streng, W. D., 43

Strietelmeyer, J., 138
Stringfellow, W., 15, 76, 138

Teresa, Saint of Avila, 31
Thielicke, H., 34, 55
Tillich, P., 5, 12, 30, 41, 92, 95, 99,
   100, 119, 121, 122, 123, 132, 134
Tournier, P., 7
Trueblood, E., 76

Van Buren, P. M., 99, 105, 124

Wagner, J. H., Jr., 64
Ward, H. H., 103
Waskow, A. I., 114
Webber, G. W., 76, 99, 125

Weber, H. R., 77
Weber, M., 100
Weber, O., 99
Weer, H. R., 97
Welch, C., 34
Westberg, G. E., 99
Whitehead, A. N., 120
Wieser, T., 94
Wilder, A. N., 6, 7
Williams, C., 15, 60, 91
Williams, D. D., 90
Wingren, G., 42, 43
Winter, G., 67, 76, 94
Wright, G. E., 34

Zimmerman, C. C., 111

Index of Subjects, Persons, and Places

Abraham, 36, 42, 48, 84
Acceptance, 122 ff.
Acts of God, 49
Adam, 18, 19, 20
Adults, religion for, 5
Agape, 35
Agenda for Church, 41
Ambiguity, doctrines, 2
Amos, 70
Anfechtung, 132
Apostles' Creed, 53
Aristotle, 16
Art, and religion, 54
Authority in morals, 105

Baptism, 84
Baptism and Instruction, 89
Bathsheba, 23
Bible
    as liturgy, 84
    body of truth, vi
    priorities within, 3
    read on own terms, 40
    study, 73
Biography of Christ, 39
Bloch, Ernst, 80

Canon, 55
    history of, 46
Catechism, vi
    new, 78
Catholic Church, 78
Celebration, 87
Charity, plantation, 21
Chastity and charity, 109
Christ
    and culture, 108
    as host, 87
    as human, 42
Christian as man, 65
Christianity,
    future of, 14
    religionless, 61

Church
    and error, 78
    as institution, 57
    as mission, 52
    building, 32
    confusion of, vi
    deadness of, 65
    divided, 79
    one, 81
    ridicule of, 81
City, inner, 77
Commandments, Ten, 2, 109, 110, 111
Commitment, price of, 55
Community action, 74
Confirmation, 86
Confrontation, 6
    escape of, 19
Constantinople, Patriarch of, 72
Consummation, 135
Contemporaneity, cult of, 120
Contemplation, 93
Covenant, 85
Creation
    affirmed, 95
    involvement in, 116
Creeds, 4
    origin of, 47
Culture and Christ, 108

Darrow, 19
David, 48, 84, 106
Death, 130
Decalogue, 2
Decision, moment of, 39
Denomination, 74
Dialog, 76
Discrimination, 74
Disease, 62
Division, in church, 3
Doubt, 5

Ecumenics, 72

151

Education
    and baptism, 85
    and guilt, 119
    as discovery, vii
    dynamic, 83, 98
    ecumenical, 74
    in ethics, 107
    paternalistic, 8
Encounter, the moment, 6
Epistles, 50
Erasmus, 90
Estrangement, of generations, 13
Ethics, contextual, 104
Eucharist, 84, 86, 90
    perversion of, 88
Euthusiasts, 62
Evangelism, 66
    abduction of, 5
Eve, 18, 19, 20
Evolution, 126
Exhibitionists, 89
Extremism, danger of, 48
Ezekiel, 70
Ezra, 82

Faith
    and culture, 50
    and love, 4
    basis of, 83
    leap of, 28
    personal, 48
    without content, 1
Fellowship, broken, 64
Flesh, 40
Form and function, 70
Frustration, 82
Futility and sin, 118

Gabriel, 23
Gandhi, 114
Garaudy, Roger, 80
Ghetto, 75
Gidon, 36
God
    a politician, 30
    as person, 26
    meaningless term, 25
Gospel
    communication of, 5
    social, 63

Groups, Small, 9
Guilt and the church, 118

Healing, 18
Health of Church, 33
Hermeneutics, 41
Hiddenness, 132
History
    and man, 20
    planned, 35
Home, heavenly, 137
Hope, theology of, 127
Human
    dignity, 115
    emphasis on, 16
Humanizing, the world, 80

Incarnation, 23
Interpretation of Bible, 46
Intoxication and Spirit, 45
Irrelevant church, 76
Isaiah, 37, 39, 49, 70
Israel, History of, 37 ff.
Issues, ultimate, 45, 51

Jacob, 113
James, 50, 135
Jeremiah, 70
Jesus, as man, 17
Jews, 78
Job, 21, 121
John, 54, 70, 135
John the Baptist, 39

Kairos, 40
Kenosis, 75
Koinonia, 72
    ethic, 116

Laity, emphasis on, 97
Language
    as barrier, 36
    bondage of, 50
    liberating, 54
Law, civil, 116
Legalist, 40
Legalistic ethics, 106
Love
    afraid to, 114
    and Spirit, 120

as basic, 4
community of, 59
in ethics, 108
Luther, from below, 12
Lutherans and Reformed, 62

Man
addressable, 18
as Christian, 23
as question, 12
creation of, 36
question of, 17
Marriage and sex, 107
Marx, Karl, 23
Marxists, 79
dialogue with, 75
Mary, 30, 45, 130
Matthew, 12, 23, 50
Megalopolis, 73
Messianic reference, 49
Minister of local church, 45
Miracles, 23
Missionaries, 60
Missions
and hope, 135
world, 66
Monotheism, 36
Morality, new, 104
Moses, 36, 49, 84
Mystery, 88
Myth, 51

New emphases, 68
Nietzsche, 17

Orthodoxy, 29

Parable, 6
Parish, 61
priorities in, 4
structure of, 70
Paul, Apostle, 6, 22, 41, 42, 63,
65, 74, 76, 88, 92, 115, 129, 135
Pentecostal, churches, 53
Perfection, vii
Peter, 44, 46, 48, 61, 62, 70, 92,
114
Peter the Great, 82
Pharisee, 33
Philip, 132
Picasso, 54

Pietism and servanthood, 68
Piety and pietism, 76
Politics in church, 62
Pollution, 115
Poverty, 113
and church, 63
Preaching as dialogue, 100
Proof passages, 40
Prophets, false, 37
Psalms, writing of, 38
Psychiatrist, 65
Psychology, limits of, 11
Public sector, 76

Questions, right, 52

Rahab, 23
Reality, good or bad, 9
Redeeming and redeemed, 69
Redemption, cosmic, 129
Reflection, 32
Reform, 124
Reformation, 59, 64
of church, 82
today, 51
Reformed and Lutheran, 62
Relationship, called to, 111
Religion
as opium, 75
established, 13
where start, 1
Religiosity, flight to, 29
Religious liberty, 77
Renewal, 77
dynamics of, 82
Restatement, of Scripture, 53
Revelation and imagination, 55
Revolution, 109, 114
scientific, 102
Rural, 77
Ruth, 23

Samson, 36
Sara, 123
Savonarola, 82
Scandal of the Gospel, 41, 51
Scripture modernized, 51
Secularism, 66
Secularization, 66
Segregation, 45
Selection, of materials, v

Self-acceptance, 23
Servanthood and pietism, 68
Sex and marriage, 107
Sexes as equal, 45
Shalom, 40
Simplicity, encounter with, 121
Sin and futility, 118
Social, 90
   changes, 55
   imperatives, 129
   issues, 4
Spirit
   and church, 58
   creative, 47
   work of, 44
Stewardship, 84
Structure
   of church, 69
   value of, 92
Suffering, 69
   unbearable, 33
Symbolism
   cf. Myth

Tamar, 23
Theology
   and social change, 64
   of change, 58
   of cross, 131

Thomas, 32
Tradition, 47
   study of, 83
Trinity, 30

Ultimates, 123
Unbeliever, works of, 23
Unity, 77

Vatican Council, 5
Virgin Birth, 12

Washington, G., 114
Walls of separation, 74
Wars for Christ, 59
Woes as laments, 123
World
   Council, 72
   start with, 11
Worldliness holy, 76
Worship
   and renewal, 83
   forms of, 41
   in truth, 61
Writings, Sacred, 38

Youth and morals, 112

Zacchaeus, 12

Index of Bible References

Genesis

.... 18
1, 3 19
1:11 54
2:7 31
3 53
3:15 .... 20, 44
19 114

Exodus

.... 53
8:22 84
33:23 131
40:34-35 23

Deuteronomy

.... 53
6:4-9, 12:6, 23:14, 26:5-11 84
30:12-14 38

2 Chronicles

7:2 23

Ezra

3:10-13 62

Job

14:18-20, 30:17-30 35
28 21

Psalms

3:4 31
8 25
23 53
33, 46:5, 92, 95, 96 84

Isaiah

.... 42
1:11-15, 42:5-8 84
11:1-9 49
34:1-3 55
40:7-8 38
42:15 132
53 44
58:1-6 23

Jeremiah

7:4 62
31:33 84

Daniel

.... 23
11:32 124

Hosea

.... 85
9:7 45

Amos

4:4, 5:21-24 84

Micah

5:5 40

Matthew

5:15, 6:34, 22:37-39 39
22:37-39 114
23:13 100
25:40 31
26:26-29 87

Mark

.... 18
2:25 f. 106
4:9 92
10:17-22 69
11:12-25 55
11:15-17 115

Luke

3:10-14, 17:21 39
11:52 100
12:16-21 20
14:28-33 113
15:20 31
22:37, 24:44 49

John

.... 42
2:19-20, 3:3-4, 4:10-11, 6:51-
52, 7:33-35, 11:11-12, 12:

32-34, 13:8-9, 14:3-5, 21:
22-23 54
5:53, 63 a 88
13:35 137
16:21 39
17 72

Acts

.... 41
.... 50
1:14 45
2 44
3:22 ff. 49
6 61
8 100
17:28 31

Romans

1 144
1:20 131
3:10, 3:23 20
5 54
8:19 102
8:24-25 128
12 52
12:1 87

1 Corinthians

6:12 106
11 90
11:26 87
11:27 ff. 88
12 .... 52, 77
13 65
13:13 134
15 133

2 Corinthians

1:22, 5:5 129
5 130

Galatians

.... 50
2:11-21 92
4:20 6

Ephesians

1:14 129
2:14, 6:15 40
2:15, 2:17 42
4 52
4:11-12 100

Philippians

2:7 75

Colossians

1 .... 96, 129
1:13-14 49
1:27 128

1 Thessalonians

4:18 130

1 Timothy

6:16 31

2 Timothy

3:12 85

Hebrews

1:1 28
3:1-7 49
11:1 134
12:29 31

1 Peter

2:9 85

Revelation

21 133
21:23 128
22:13 130